P9-DFC-745

Graduate Students

Graduate Students

EXPERIENCE AT COLUMBIA UNIVERSITY, 1940-1956

By HANS ROSENHAUPT

with the assistance of THOMAS J. CHINLUND

NEW YORK 1958

COLUMBIA UNIVERSITY PRESS

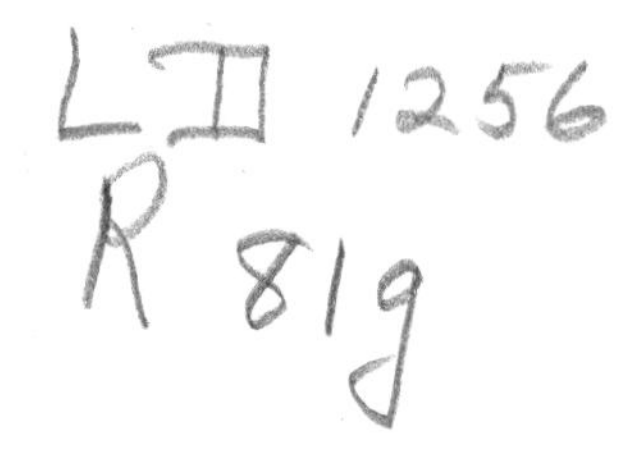

PUBLISHED IN GREAT BRITAIN, CANADA, INDIA, AND PAKISTAN
BY THE OXFORD UNIVERSITY PRESS
LONDON, TORONTO, BOMBAY, AND KARACHI

MANUFACTURED IN THE UNITED STATES OF AMERICA

LIBRARY OF CONGRESS CATALOG CARD NUMBER 58:59505

ACKNOWLEDGMENTS

WITHOUT research grants generously given and then supplemented by the Fund for the Advancement of Education, a division of the Ford Foundation, this study could not have been undertaken. To Dean Jacques Barzun, for his unfailing interest in the completion of this study and his numerous improvements in the form of the final manuscript, I am particularly indebted.

A few of the many graduate students at Columbia who helped must be mentioned by name: C. Lawson Crowe assisted in the first planning; Jean Celli Doherty and John Groppe organized and supervised the gathering of data in 1956 and 1957; and Thomas J. Chinlund in 1957 and 1958 evaluated the data with great skill and enduring patience. The staffs and facilities of the Watson Scientific Computing Laboratory, the Bureau of Applied Social Research, and the Institute of Psychological Research, all at Columbia University, were often called upon and never failed us. Joseph Nemesi of IBM, Frank Bowles of the College Entrance Examination Board, David Robertson of Barnard College, and Charles Cole, then of Columbia, now Dean of Lafayette College; Dean Peter Elder and Dean Reginald Phelps of Harvard, Dean John Fagg of New York University, Dr. Lester Evans of the Commonwealth Fund, and Dean Moody Prior of Northwestern University were interested in the study and helped generously with suggestions. The same is true of many at Columbia: Professors Marjorie Nicolson, Arthur Macmahon, Ernest Simmons, Charles Behre, Charles Frankel, Herbert Robbins, Fred Croxton, Paul Lazarsfeld, Charles Glock, Irving Lorge, Wallace Eckert, and Karl Bigelow; also John Mullins, Charles Hurd, David Evans, Madeline Dignus, and Elizabeth Levers of the Registrar's and Bursar's offices; Clara Shapiro,

Sidney Spivack, Tom Banta, and Helmut Guttenberg of the Bureau of Applied Social Research; and Henry Wiggins and Vergene Leverenz of Columbia University Press. All these and many others had a share in the making of this book. I am responsible for its shortcomings.

HANS ROSENHAUPT

Princeton, New Jersey
October 15, 1958

CONTENTS

TABLES

APPENDIX

Graduate Students

Chapter One. INTRODUCTION

TODAY, when the American public discusses higher education with passion, a book about the graduate student's origins, support, and career may be offered without apology. Finding out more than we know today about students who have pursued their education beyond college will indeed help us in making decisions about their recruitment, training, and support. Is it, for example, sound policy to attract more women into graduate education? Do very young college graduates make successful graduate students and, if so, should we shorten the time which bright young men and women now spend in college? Do certain colleges fail to prepare their seniors for graduate work? How does a large-scale program of support affect graduate students? The answers to these and similar questions are of more than academic interest.

For better or worse, our nation finds itself elevated, within the memory of one generation, to a position of world leadership. Our influence has not been gained by political or military conquest. Rather, through complex events the United States has reached a level of industrial, financial, and military strength which makes her potential preceptor to the world. Whether we want to be preceptors is not the issue at this point, but whether we will so to speak conduct ourselves in a manner befitting our station.

America's ability to lead, of course, concerns every man and woman who enters a polling booth, but more especially those whose job it is to guide our schools, elementary and secondary, our colleges, and our graduate schools. Through organized education an overwhelming majority of our people may be reached, and whatever changes need to be made are most easily effected by reforms at the top of our educational pyramid, in our graduate schools. Here are trained the college professors who have a decisive influence on approximately one fourth of our population—

those generally considered most intelligent, most ambitious, most active in our national life. Indirectly the pace is set here for the high schools. High school graduates must meet the standards established by the colleges, and colleges in turn are bound to follow the graduate schools where basic research is carried on, where new and fresh thoughts are born and fostered. In short, the intellectual, moral and technological solutions to the problems of our day are sought in the world of graduate education.

Unfortunately there are always leaders of opinion or makers of decisions in government, foundations, and educational institutions who are not prepared for change. Their indifference or resistance is largely due to ignorance. The President's Committee on Education beyond the High School spoke more than once to this point in its 1957 Report:

"We have been struck above all else by the astounding lack of accurate, consistent, and up-to-date facts, and by how little this Nation knows about its enormously vital and expensive educational enterprise in contrast to how it knows, in great detail, about agriculture, industry, labor, banking and other areas . . . . Until the gross deficiencies in educational reporting are remedied, all advisory work, all research, all educational planning throughout the country and all efforts by individual States, communities and institutions to devise effective actions will be severely handicapped." [1]

It is literally true that today we know next to nothing about the supply of and demand for graduate students, or about their careers while in graduate school. We have some knowledge about the number of years certain students took to acquire their Ph.D.'s, but as yet no large-scale study of the successes and failures of graduate students, their origins, their ages, or their support exists. To be sure, no single study can supply all the information we need for sound decisions, nor can anybody identify all the factors that influence the selection and training of young men and women who attend the graduate schools of the United States. But we do need intensive studies of limited areas in order to make more comprehensive treatments possible.

Foundations, organizations, and federal agencies, recognizing the need for more knowledge, have in the past few years subsidized studies of particular aspects of graduate education, such as the baccalaureate origins of doctorates, the financial support of graduate education, or the personnel policies of colleges and universities. In doing so, they have reflected the general interest in higher education, an interest which has two particular sources. First, the American people have recently found themselves short of highly trained men, especially scientists, engineers, and linguists. Second, it is now generally known that beginning in the early 1960s a flood of students will pour into our colleges. We shall then desperately need more college teachers—possibly double the number now in service.

No doubt some of the voices that warn us today sound strident. Our need for skilled manpower is sometimes exaggerated; shortages are aggravated by the misuse and hoarding of experts; the dramatic appearance of "Sputnik" has roused an interest which may prove as short-lived as Sputnik itself; the flood of college students has not yet materialized. Yet our power can always be threatened by new technical developments, and our precarious position of guardianship can be challenged by nations whose intelligence is better trained and better utilized than ours. How we educate our children and young people is thus not an academic matter but one of survival.

At first glance our graduate schools may give the impression that since their establishment eighty years ago we have achieved the best possible education beyond college. Graduate education occupies the energies of a much larger number of our people today than ever before. In 1870 there were only 44 graduate students in America; there were 2,400 in 1890; today the number is about a quarter of a million. The 25 institutions offering graduate programs in 1876 increased to 270 in the 1920s, and to 615 in 1955–56.[2] Of the 411,058 earned degrees conferred in 1956–57, 61,955, or 15.1 percent, were master's degrees; 8,756, or 2.1 percent, were doctoral degrees.[3]

But the hundredfold growth of our graduate student population since 1900 does not mean that we have increased our devotion to higher learning a hundredfold. First, the entire population has increased from 75,994,575 in 1900 to 175 million. Second, the college population has grown from 237,592 to 3,068,417. This increase means that a larger share of the college-age population, those between 18 and 21, attends college. In 1900, only 4 percent of the college-age group went to college, whereas today about 25 percent do, and some people believe that eventually almost half of this entire age group will attend college for at least two years. Third, the spectacular rise in the number of graduate students is caused largely by the increased need for elementary and secondary school teachers; this need is heightened by the fact that to an evergrowing extent teachers on the secondary level are expected to hold at least a master's degree. The relative increase in graduate students is therefore spectacular only at the level of master's degree candidates; it is modest at the doctoral level. The number of master's degrees given in 1900 was about one-sixteenth the number of bachelor's degrees awarded that year; today it is about one-fifth. The number of doctor's degrees in 1900 was about one-sixtieth the number of bachelor's degrees; today the number is about one-thirtieth.

Again, quantitative growth at any level does not entail qualitative superiority. In the nineteenth century, for example, when a much smaller percentage of the population attended high school, over 60 percent of high school graduates continued through college, as against under 15 percent today. Similarly, in the early part of our century a college education stood for a higher and more specialized kind of learning than it does now. The quantitative increase in graduate study may be caused by a general lowering of college requirements: to reach a level of specialized knowledge equal to, say, a British honor's bachelor's degree, students must complete at least one year beyond college and earn a master's degree.

Large figures, because it is hard to visualize what they represent have a dulling and thus comforting effect. We can conjure up the sight of a field army of highly trained students leaving our graduate schools every year—an army equal to five or six standard infantry divisions of ten thousand. But even this great force does not meet all our needs for advanced researchers and college teachers. More than half of the 61,955 master's degrees in 1956–57 were awarded to men and women in secondary education, and more than twelve thousand to those in professional fields such as engineering, business, agriculture, and theology. Master's degrees in liberal arts and sciences thus accounted for less than one-third of the total degrees or somewhat less than twenty thousand. Similarly, only a little more than five thousand of the approximate nine thousand doctoral degrees were awarded in disciplines which are traditionally thought of as college and pure research subjects. And we know that only a fraction of those earning Ph.D.'s in liberal arts enter college teaching. During the 1930s, for example, higher education got no more than 60 percent of the new Ph.D.'s.[4]

The need for college teachers is already so great that the output of our graduate schools fails to meet the demand. As a result, professional standards have been lowered deplorably. The proportion of college teachers with Ph.D.'s has dropped, that of college teachers without even an M.A. has risen (see page 91).

The outlook for the immediate future is distressing for an additional reason. The large population group born in the 1940s which will enter our colleges in the 1960s was preceded by a relatively small generation born in the 1930s, the very generation which must supply young college teachers for the populous generation born ten years later. Depending on assumptions we make about the future, the need for new college teachers in the year 1960 will be between seventeen and twenty-four thousand, and in the year 1970 between twenty-five and thirty thousand.[5] Even the most optimistic projection for doctoral degrees in liberal arts subjects to be awarded in the next ten years do not come near the figure of ten thousand per year. Therefore fewer and fewer colleges will be able to renew and enlarge their staff with Ph.D.'s. By 1970, only 20 percent of college teachers may hold Ph.D.'s, as against 40 percent today.[6]

The following facts and thoughts about the graduate student, his origins, his career, his success, his failures, and his future are associated with the division of Columbia University in which master's and doctor's programs in the liberal arts and sciences are offered, namely the three Graduate Faculties of Political Science, Philosophy, and Pure Science. These faculties, formally established between 1875 and 1892, have contributed and continue to contribute a sizable number to the national total of Ph.D. degrees.

Between the years 1861 and 1955, Columbia University awarded nine thousand, seven hundred and eleven doctorates, 8.5 percent of the country's total for those years. In 1957 the University awarded 6.0 percent of that year's total. Table 1 shows Columbia's share in

Table 1. COLUMBIA'S SHARE IN THE NATION'S PRODUCTION OF PH.D.'S IN FOURTEEN MAJOR FIELDS, BY PERIODS

	1936–56		*1936–42*		*1943–49*		*1950–56*	
Field	*Number*	*Percent*	*Number*	*Percent*	*Number*	*Percent*	*Number*	*Percent*
Chemistry	500	3.5	170	4.7	161	4.5	169	2.4
Geology and other earth sciences	170	8.9	33	7.3	40	10.8	97	8.9
Mathematics	77	2.9	19	3.3	21	3.8	37	2.4
Physics and astronomy	192	3.4	41	3.8	29	2.9	122	3.5
Zoology	102	3.5	29	3.7	22	3.6	51	3.4
Psychology	235	4.1	92	11.3	71	8.3	72	1.7 *
Anthropology and archaeology	114	18.1	25	14.3	17	13.5	72	22.0
Economics	254	6.7	66	7.9	61	8.3	127	5.7
History	407	9.6	110	9.8	99	11.0	198	8.9
Sociology	134	6.9	33	8.6	24	6.0	77	6.7
English language and literature	300	7.1	72	6.2	64	7.2	164	7.7
Foreign languages and literature	386	11.5	106	8.9	84	11.5	196	13.6
Philosophy	183	14.6	56	16.2	37	13.9	90	14.1
Religion	86	4.2	no figures for Columbia		15	2.3	71	7.5

Source: M. H. Trytten and L. R. Harmon, *Doctorate Production in United States Universities 1936–1956, with Baccalaureate Origins of Doctorates in Sciences, Arts, and Humanities* (Publication 582, National Academy of Sciences–National Research Council, Washington, D. C., 1958).

* In this period the *national* production of Ph.D.'s in psychology increased out of proportion to the growth in other fields.

the years 1936 to 1956 in the nation's production of Ph.D.'s in fifteen major fields. In comparing Columbia's particular share in the three time periods listed, it is helpful to remember that the country's entire production of Ph.D.'s in the two periods 1936–42 and 1943–49 was around twenty thousand but rose to fifty-six thousand in the interval of 1950 to 1956. This major rise accounts for some relative decreases in Columbia's share.

The Graduate Faculties of Columbia University during the years 1940–56 received every year an entering class representative of every region of the United States as well as of many foreign countries, and, at the same time, of metropolitan New York. Roughly speaking, one-third of each entering class consisted of natives of New York City; one-fourth came from New England and the Middle Atlantic states, one-fifth from the rest of the country, and the remainder from foreign lands. Slightly more than half of the foreign students had received their college degrees in the United States.

By virtue of its composition, then, Columbia's graduate school is of special interest. It attracts both full-time graduate students, who often come from a distance, and local students, who often earn their degrees by attending school part time. After the Second World War, Columbia University attracted large numbers of veterans, whose records afford an opportunity to study the success of a program of government subsidy. Furthermore, the Graduate Faculties, especially the Faculty of Philosophy, have always accepted many women students; we can thus learn a good deal about a group which may play an important part in the expansion of graduate education in the future. Finally, Columbia tolerates within her walls great differences of policy as regards the administration of programs, from closely supervised and prescribed studies in one department to freedom reminiscent of continental universities in another. This affords interesting comparisons of methods through their effect on success and failure as well as on the time needed for the completion of degrees.

In order to obtain data, well over thirty thousand records of students registered under Columbia's Graduate Faculties were studied. As may be seen in Table 51, almost twenty-four thousand of these tabulated records were of students who entered the Graduate Faculties between 1940 and 1955; this number was about 90 percent of the actual total entering during those years for whom the Registrar had kept a permanent record. The study excluded students who were not entered in an academic degree program, particularly those in special army and navy programs during the Second World War, those for whom not enough data were available, and also a small percentage of students whose records were temporarily out of the files when photographing for the study was undertaken.

The study also included the records of 3,972 students who had entered the Graduate Faculties before 1940, but who were still registered or obtained a degree between 1940 and 1956. Finally, the study tabulated 2,270 records representing a 10 percent sample of all those who studied in the Graduate Faculties before 1940, most of them during the 1930s and a few during the 1920s. Records for students who attended in the earlier part of the century are generally kept in a form which made photographing impracticable.

Generally, the omitted records belonged to students who were not serious enough about their graduate work to submit undergraduate transcripts showing the award of their degrees and whose records in the Registrar's office were thus incomplete. On the other hand, a careful check of Ph.D. holders was made, so that the survey included over 99 percent of those who were awarded Ph.D.'s between 1940 and Commencement 1956.

The following data from the Registrar's records were coded and punched on IBM cards: Year and state or country of birth, sex and military status, undergraduate college and date of undergraduate degree, year and semester of entrance to the Graduate Faculties, department of major interest (and area studies Institute if appropriate), point loads in each of the semesters and summer sessions during the first five years, type and date of graduate degree or institute certificate obtained.

Furthermore, a total of all points taken was computed for all students except those registered during the academic year 1955–56, as well as the extent to which students had taken graduate courses before being formally admitted to graduate work.

Photographing and coding of the Registrar's records were done by graduate students and checked carefully. Punching was done by trained keyboard operators and spotchecked. Many tests of the accuracy of the data were made, and a maximum error of 3 percent in a difficult column was found. Since the errors appeared to be random, and since most breakdowns dealt with large numbers of cases, this error did not interfere with the validity of our findings. Wherever coding and punching errors may have had a bearing on the findings, the reader's attention will be called to that fact.

The careers described in the following chapters seem to resemble one another in many ways. A large majority of the Ph.D.'s, for example, were earned in periods of between four and seven years. The ratio of success (earning a degree) and failure was apt to be in the neighborhood of 50 percent. And, while the small variations in these large patterns are interesting, the similarities between the several groups are more striking than the differences. However, to conclude from these patterns that individual graduate students resemble one another would be a mistake. Graduate students do in fact differ widely in age, background, motivation, and attitude toward their studies. Columbia's Graduate Faculties have over the years been home to men and women nearly as different from one another as the people in any group picked at random—some remarkably different from the average: an Iowa youth who came to Columbia to prepare himself for college teaching and who returned to his old college as soon as he had obtained his degree; a rabbi who during almost forty years attended one course a semester without ever earning a degree; a young genius who completed his doctoral work in two years; a rich young woman who intended merely to spend a pleasant year in New York but was introduced to the writings of an obscure author and stayed in graduate study for many years; a bluestocking who came determined to earn a Ph.D. degree but left after one year of graduate study to get married; a public relations expert who entered the Graduate Faculties in a mood similar to that of a sinner entering a monastery; an unsuccessful author who resigned himself to earning his "union card" as a college teacher; a retired chemical engineer who finally had time to do what he liked to do best, study Homer.

Many students entered graduate school immediately after college; others were in their late twenties when they started because they had served their country in uniform or held a job; some were in their fifties and even a few in their sixties. Most graduate students are serious about their studies, but some are not. Some like music, others art; some read widely outside their fields, others as little as possible. Few are athletic, but some are. Many are poor and must be careful with their money, but a few are rich. Many dress simply or even carelessly, but a few look dapper. The only features the majority have in common are independence of mind and self-reliance, a deep interest in their field of study, and a determination to pass through their period of apprenticeship successfully and rapidly, so that the rewards at the end—a job, prestige, a promotion—may be reaped.

What is true of Columbia's graduate students is true everywhere—no single image of the graduate student can be drawn. Unlike professional graduate students, liberal arts graduate students lack even the equalizing influence of a common fate. A law student knows beforehand that he must spend exactly three years in law school, a medical student that he must spend four in medical school. Not so the graduate student outside the professions. If everything goes extremely well, he may receive a doctor's degree two or three years after leaving college. But he may have trouble passing the certifying examinations, or his dissertation may not satisfy his sponsor, or he may be too preoccupied by teaching and family cares to progress in his research; ten or even twenty years may pass before the degree is awarded. And while certain patterns prevail in certain departments, the best anyone can do is to guess how long it may take a student after entering graduate school, or even after passing his certifying examination, to earn his doctorate.

Moreover, professional students in law or medicine or education have in common a clearly defined vocational goal and are preparing themselves for standardized professional examinations; they must take prescribed courses, and can thus be more justly thought of as poured into a common mold. No professional examinations for college teachers await graduate students; and the university examinations, especially for the Ph.D., differ widely from one graduate school, one department, and one individual to another. They differ in scope and in particular content. Even if there were professional examinations for college teachers, a large number, in some disciplines more than half, of graduate students have no intention of becoming college teachers. Some hope to enter government service, others research or administrative jobs in industry or elsewhere, still others simply attend graduate school for the pleasure of pursuing advanced study.

It is as hard to define a graduate school as it is to describe a typical graduate student. The graduate school seems far removed from the concerns of the average man and woman, a place vaguely associated with difficult mathematical formulas, languages so rare that only a few professors know them, research methods so refined and complex that outsiders must despair of even understanding what is being measured. The public is further confused by the fact that the graduate school is simultaneously a professional school training college teachers and a company of scholars advancing pure research.

The term "graduate education" encompasses widely diversified areas of human endeavor: literature and languages, political science, history and economics, physics and chemistry and biology, old and venerable subjects such as philosophy and mathematics, relatively new fields such as psychology, sociology, anthropology, statistics, and biochemistry, and highly specialized disciplines such as the study of exotic and extinct languages, or of human variation, or of biophysics. Graduate work furthermore touches many so-called professional fields. The *Guide to Graduate Study*,[7] recently published by the Association of American Colleges and based on answers to questionnaires, includes fields, such as education, which in some universities are departments and in others (e.g. Columbia) are part of a distinct professional school.

While certain particular properties of Columbia's graduate school will emerge from the descriptive tabulations later on, a few should be mentioned here. The school is organized into three fairly independent faculties—Political Science, Philosophy, and Pure Science—which accounts for its official name, the Graduate Faculties, rather than "the Graduate School." All three faculties make the same basic requirements for the degrees: registration for 30 semester hours or points for the master's degree and 60 points for the doctor's degree. There are no university regulations against part-time attendance, but many departments, notably in the Faculty of Pure Science, prefer students who can attend full time.

A candidate for the doctor's degree may receive up to 30 points of credit toward the 60 required points for work taken at another graduate school. In contrast to most other graduate schools, the Graduate Faculties sets no limit upon the time during which a student may be a candidate for either degree. But students who have been absent for more than five years must go through the process of formal readmission at which time they may lose previously earned credits; they are not usually penalized unless the absence has been so long as to have made the preparation obsolete.

Students are generally admitted to the Graduate Faculties without being specifically labeled as prospective M.A. or Ph.D. candidates. Those who enter directly from college—the large majority—generally earn a master's degree on the way to the Ph.D., but some by-pass it (see Tables 44 and 45). Some departments supervise their students closely in order to be able to advise them whether or not they should continue beyond the first year as prospective candidates for the doctorate. However, the weeding out before the second or even third year, in spite of sincere efforts, is not always effective in deterring unpromising students (see p. 87).

Course requirements for the master's degree are naturally more precise than those for the doctorate, which, in spite of the large numbers involved, has remained a degree bestowed upon an individual for a particular and unique combination of abilities demonstrated in a particular program of courses, examinations, and research. It is therefore difficult to generalize about requirements for the doctorate.

Columbia's oldest graduate faculty, Political Science, today consists of six departments: Anthropology, Economics, History, Mathematical Statistics, Public Law and Government (this department in most graduate schools would be called "Political Science"), and Sociology. With the exception of Anthropology, all these departments are housed in the same university building, and generally there is close cooperation among them. The faculty requires that 21 points of the 30 needed for the master's degree be taken for examination credit. This credit, unlike the mere attendance or registration credit, is given when a student has completed the required work in a course, including a final examination or paper.

Nine points of the 30 required for the master's degree may be earned by registering for courses without writing a paper or taking an examination.

Master's essays are required by all departments in the Political Science faculty; the departments of History and Public Law and Government also require reading knowledge of one foreign language. Two languages are needed for the Ph.D., except in Economics, Sociology, and Public Law, which in recent years have allowed substitution of mathematics for one language.

The requirements for degrees in the six departments are virtually the same, and students and teachers cross departmental boundaries without difficulty. Supervision of students varies not only from department to department, but also within a department, according to a candidate's field of specialization.

Virtually all decisions on admissions are made in the University Office of Admissions, and since departments in the faculty rarely set numerical limits, all qualified applicants usually obtain admission. When need dictates, departments resort to such screening devices as special examinations and committees, especially for prospective Ph.D. candidates.

The Faculty of Philosophy, or, in modern terminology, that of humanities, is more diversified than the Faculty of Political Science. Its largest department, English and Comparative Literature, accounts for roughly half of all students in the faculty. Language departments include Chinese and Japanese, Germanic Languages, Greek and Latin, Near and Middle East Languages (until recently called Semitic Languages), Slavic Languages, a newly founded department of Uralic and Altaic Languages, and Romance Languages; the last, to all intents and purposes, consists of three separate departments, French and Romance Philology, Spanish, and Italian. The remaining departments in this faculty are Fine Arts and Archaeology, Linguistics, Music, and Philosophy. The master's and doctor's programs in religion are administered by standing committees of instructors from Union Theological Seminary and the Columbia Graduate Faculties, but for the purpose of this descriptive survey Religion has been listed as a department in the Faculty of Philosophy.

Like the Faculty of Political Science, the Faculty of Philosophy, with the exception of the English department, generally requires 21 points of examination credits for the master's degree and 9 for registration (attendance) credit. Individual differences will be mentioned whenever they may account for significant statistical differences. Since about one-sixth and sometimes one-fifth of the entire graduate population are English majors, it is important to remember that, unlike any other department in the Graduate Faculties, the English department requires no course examination credits whatever. Like students at a continental university, candidates for the M.A. and Ph.D. in English demonstrate mastery of their subject in comprehensive final examinations toward the end of their studies.

Admissions to English, Philosophy, French, German, Greek and Latin, and Spanish are made in the Office of University Admissions. The other departments choose their candidates themselves. With the exception of the highly selective Music and Religion departments, admission is generally granted to all qualified applicants. Some few departments admit probationary students. At times, and notably in the late 1940s, the larger departments, such as English, were overcrowded. This was felt to be a necessary sacrifice to accommodate the numerous returning veterans.

The Faculty of Pure Science comprises eight departments on the 116th Street campus: Astronomy, Botany, Chemistry, Geology, Mathematics, Physics, Psychology, and Zoology; and six departments connected with the College of Physicians and Surgeons at 168th Street: Anatomy, Biochemistry, Microbiology, Pathology, Pharmacology, and Physiology. Furthermore, six Engineering departments—Chemical, Civil, Electrical, Industrial, Mechanical, and Mining, Metallurgical and Mineral—offer Ph.D. degrees under the auspices of the Graduate Faculties and, for the purposes of the Ph.D. program, belong in the Faculty of Pure Science.

Pure Science by the very nature of its work in the laboratory can maintain closer supervision of its students than the two other faculties. Credit toward any degree is given only for courses in which examinations have been passed, or for supervised research in the laboratory. Admission to research is granted only when at least one professor is well acquainted with the student and when performance in the first year has been thoroughly satisfactory.

Admission is made by the department; because of laboratory space, numbers are limited. As will be seen in Chapter Four, the Faculty of Pure Science is able to offer its graduate students financial support to a larger extent than are the other two faculties.

This study does not undertake to establish correlations between the quality of undergraduate and graduate performance, for it is not feasible to compare the widely varying grading habits of colleges. Furthermore, some departments at Columbia report no letter grades, such as A or B or F, to the Registrar. The English department requires no grades, students in the Faculties of Philosophy and Political Science beyond the master's level generally take courses either for R (registration) credit or, in seminars and colloquia, receive a "pass" or "fail." A uniform scale for transposing the letter grades that are given would be hard to construct. The medical science departments following the severe grading scheme of the medical school, give out more low marks than other departments, and individual instructors in fields such as Public Law or Religion may similarly be influenced by the grading pattern of the professional school with which they are affiliated. In this study, therefore, success has been defined simply as the attainment of a degree; the imponderable and slight differences in quality of undergraduate preparation have been disregarded.

All students who entered before the war, left, and returned as veterans were treated as veterans. Although relatively few in number, these students were more successful in obtaining graduate degrees than any other group studied.

Undoubtedly further conclusions as to the significance of particular factors and combinations of factors for predicting success could be drawn from our data, but the present survey attempts only broad statements based on large groups. Whenever possible, averages and percentages were based on groups of at least fifty students; when it was necessary to base them on smaller numbers, that fact is noted.

Data on the Ed.D. and the Ph.D. in education were not included because (1) the Ph.D. program in education is virtually autonomous, and (2) the very large number of M.A. candidates in education could not be considered in this study since the degree is completely administered and supervised by the faculty of Teachers College. It is hoped that a separate study of graduate students in education will be undertaken.

Chapter Two. COLLEGES OF BACCALAUREATE ORIGIN AND AREAS OF BIRTH

IN THE LAST pages of his *Age of Constantine the Great,* Jacob Burckhardt depicts the fierce competition for students in fourth-century Athens. "The very arrival of the student was a perilous affair; at the Piraeus, if he had not already been encountered at the headland of Sunium, men stood ready to watch for new students in order to recruit them for one or another lecture hall, even employing threats to change a decision which the student might already have taken at home. Teachers suddenly appeared at the harbor to make sure of their prey. If a man got safely to Athens, perhaps under the protection of the ship's captain, he found himself exposed to actual violence; not infrequently there were assault, murder, and consequent criminal investigations, and all because of the rivalry of teachers." [1]

In twentieth-century America methods of recruitment are less direct, but under a veneer of urbanity passions still burn, as all those admissions officers can testify who have suffered a department's wrath when a promising candidate—usually a potential chemist—has got away.

Actually the shortage of graduate students is no laughing matter, and the shortage of *well qualified* ones is serious, though little is said and less written about it. Why? Nobody wants to discourage the brave souls who, qualified or not, are now in graduate schools; and our age, which later generations may dub the Age of the Soft Pedal, suspects any criticism of ineptness, lack of intelligence, or shiftlessness. But the main reason why observers prefer to remain silent on the critical shortage of graduate students is the same lack of reliable information which we encounter everywhere. Are today's graduate students really less able than previous generations, or are our graduate teachers simply nostalgic? If students are provably less good, in what respects? Are they less well prepared? Less highly motivated? Less idealistic? Less intelligent? A student of statistics points out that the average of intelligence goes down as larger percentages of the population are drawn upon. If the shortage is so critical, where can we turn for relief? Do large-scale graduate fellowship programs such as those under Title Four of the 1958 National Defense Education Act, National Science Foundation, or the Woodrow Wilson National Fellowship Foundation, succeed in recruiting students who would otherwise not have entered graduate work? And if it can be shown that these programs succeed, are we robbing Peter—law and medical schools, teachers colleges, graduate schools of business and of engineering—to pay Paul? With our present knowledge, we cannot even attempt to answer any of these simple queries.

One question about the supply of graduate students to which at least partial answers can be given is their undergraduate origin. The Office of Scientific Personnel of the National Academy of Sciences and the National Research Council in 1958 published *Doctorates Production in United States Universities 1936–1956,* which summarizes the findings of two earlier studies (*Baccalaureate Origins of the Science Doctorates* and *Baccalaureate Origins of Doctorates in the Arts, Humanities and Social Sciences*) and brings them up to date. All three studies list Ph.D.'s by fields of study and by colleges of undergraduate origin, and the two earlier studies establish a rating order among colleges according to the actual numbers of alumni who had earned Ph.D.'s by 1950. To obtain an insight into the relative productivity of particular colleges, it would be necessary to correlate the actual numbers of Ph.D.'s with the size of those graduating college classes which may be considered as likely sources. To establish such figures, however, is difficult, because Ph.D.'s in the sciences in a given year will tend to come from more recent college classes than Ph.D.'s in the humanities and the social sciences.

In *The Younger American Scholar* (Chicago, 1953), Robert H. Knapp and Joseph J. Greenbaum attempted not only to list colleges whose graduates obtained doctor's degrees or other academic honors, but, by allowing for the relative sizes of graduating classes, to establish a relative order of merit. Another study was undertaken in 1935 at the University of Minnesota,[2] primarily to determine the relation between success of graduate students and the accreditation of their colleges of origin. No such relation was found where the completion of all graduate work was considered the criterion of success, but graduates of colleges on the accredited list of the Association of American Universities tended to be more successful than graduates of other colleges in obtaining advanced degrees. The author of the study warned that this criterion of success should not be used alone, because it might be influenced by such factors as financial ability to continue graduate study.[3]

The appended roster by states (Table 52) of all the undergraduate institutions from which students entered the Graduate Faculties of Columbia University between 1940 and 1956 lists by name only those institutions from which five or more students came, but the total number of institutions in each state or country from which students came to Columbia is indicated in parentheses. After the name of an institution are listed first the total number of its alumni entering the Graduate Faculties between 1940 and *1956,* then all Ph.D.'s earned before July, 1956, by alumni who entered between 1940 and *1950,* and finally all M.A.'s earned before July, 1956, by alumni who entered between 1940 and *1956.* In the count of Ph.D.'s, those earned by students entering after 1950 were omitted, because only 126 students in those entering classes had earned degrees by 1956 and a disproportionate number of those—87—were in the Faculty of Pure Science. Since certain colleges furnish disproportionately large contingents of scientists, a listing including these recent candidates would have distorted the picture.

The 23,498 students who entered the Graduate Faculties between 1940 and 1956 and who were included in our study came from 451 foreign colleges and universities and about 910 institutions in the United States. These figures are not accurate, because relatively numerous mistakes were made in the coding of colleges. Furthermore, the information on the colleges of undergraduate degree was itself not always accurate. Occasionally also—as for example in the case of colleges with identical names—it was ambiguous. Therefore the figures should be accepted with some reservation. They are published because they afford at least a general impression.

The full roster of all students on which Table 52 (page 105) is based is being kept in the Office of University Admissions of Columbia University, and might well be used as basis for a more detailed study. It would, for example, be useful to find out why three of the nine Ph.D.'s earned by University of Pittsburgh graduates were in the small field of botany; or why five of Brown University's six Ph.D.'s were in science fields, three of Vanderbilt's five in the department of Public Law and Government, seven of the thirteen from the University of Texas in Economics, or both of the two from Washington and Lee and four of the five from Wheaton College in Illinois in Geology. Here as in other detailed studies the great importance of individual college teachers' sending students to graduate school, or graduate professors attracting them to the graduate school where they are teaching (this happens to be the explanation for Wheaton) would have to be stressed.

Also useful would be a clearer understanding of a phenomenon which might be called the David and Jonathan syndrome—the fact that often two students entering from the same institution in the same year both succeed. It would be good to know how well pairs of the opposite sex who enter together succeed. Studies in the sociology of education which are currently being made at the University of California and at other institutions may find the Columbia data helpful in showing the relative importance for academic success of the human climate.

The list may show that graduates from college *B* succeed in earning graduate degrees, whereas graduates from colleges *A* and *C* are notably less successful. From this a naïve observer concludes that college *B* must be superior. But the sophisticated reader recalls that the tables are *not* about the graduates of colleges *A, B,* and *C,* but only about those graduates—never more than a small percentage of any graduating class—who for one reason or another, between 1940 and 1956, chose to apply and were then admitted to a Columbia graduate department. If the admitting officers or committees had all been endowed with second sight, the performances of graduates from different colleges should be identically good. One can say, with some justification, that the relative differences in performance reflect on the shortcomings of the admitters (of whom the author was one). There are good reasons for the discrepancies. Since college *A* is part of a university with its own flourishing graduate school, its top graduates continue in the university with the result that all other graduate schools, including Columbia, see only its *beaux restes.* College *C,* on the other hand, has no graduate school nearby, but since all its faculty comes from graduate schools other than Columbia, its outstanding seniors are rarely sent there; the few who enter Columbia are typically employed in downtown New York City, attend only part time, and are relatively unsuccessful in earning degrees. Conversely, college *B* is not far from Columbia University and is staffed by many Columbia Ph.D.'s who send their best students back to Columbia; furthermore, since many seniors from *B* seek entrance into Columbia, admissions committees at Columbia make the common and understandable mistake of applying stricter selective standards toward college *B* than toward colleges *A* and *C,* so that *B*'s contingent is a more carefully selected and thus a better group.

For several reasons, which have nothing to do with *B*'s quality, the group at Columbia from college *B* performs in a superior fashion, even though, by objective measures, institutions *A* and *C* are superior to *B*.

It has been claimed [4] that out-of-state and foreign students anywhere are of high quality and that the proportion of the former receiving advanced degrees is greater than among students attending institutions in their home state. Out-of-state students might conceivably be a better group for reasons which have nothing to do with the quality of their college: (1) leaving one's home state may show superior energy and initiative; (2) a willingness to sacrifice for graduate work by accepting surroundings that are less familiar and possibly more expensive than those at home may require a measure of dedication which in the long run is reflected in high performance; (3) since a graduate student away from home is removed from opportunities for part-time work, he may be apt to devote more time to his studies than the commuting student.

In the following paragraphs we refer to the *groups* of graduates from out-of-state institutions as out of state students, although a few, rarely over 20 percent, were New York residents who after their undergraduate experience out of state returned home.

If the earning of a doctor's degree is a measure of success, then claims for the out-of-state students cannot be supported by our findings. Thirteen percent of Columbia College and 11 percent of CCNY graduates had obtained doctorates by 1956, but so had California's 13 percent and Harvard's 11 percent, disregarding the 126 doctorates earned by those who entered after 1950. On the other hand, only 5 percent of graduates of Fordham (in New York City) and the University of Wisconsin earned Ph.D.'s.

Table 2 lists institutions or groups of institutions sending large numbers of graduates who by 1956 had earned Ph.D. degrees to Columbia's Graduate Faculties between 1940 and 1956:

Table 2. INSTITUTIONS OR GROUPS OF INSTITUTIONS SENDING LARGE NUMBERS OF GRADUATES TO COLUMBIA GRADUATE FACULTIES 1940–56, PH.D. DEGREES EARNED BY 1956 (*In descending order by percent*)

Institution	*Percent*	*Institution*	*Percent*
Columbia College	13	Rutgers University	6
California, University of	13	Other Middle Atlantic institutions	6
College of the City of New York	11	Barnard College	5
Harvard College	11	Other institutions in New York state	5
Foreign institutions	10	Wisconsin, University of	5
Cornell University	9	Columbia University School of General Studies	4*
Yale University	8	Vassar College	4
Other New England institutions	8	Hunter College, New York	3
Michigan, University of	8	New York University	3
Other Western institutions	8	Wellesley College	3
Queens College, New York	7		
Smith College	7		
Southern institutions	7		
Brooklyn College	6		

* Since this division sent disproportionately large numbers in recent years, the percentage is misleading. See Table 5.

Actually the differences in the ratios of success, since they are often based on small numbers, may be caused by chance. When large numbers of graduates from groups of colleges are compared the differences become surprisingly small. Of the total of 23,498 students surveyed who entered Columbia's Graduate Faculties be-

Table 3. INSTITUTIONS OR GROUPS OF INSTITUTIONS SENDING LARGE NUMBERS OF GRADUATES TO COLUMBIA GRADUATE FACULTIES 1940–50, M.A. OR PH.D. DEGREES EARNED BY 1956 (*In percent*)

		Ph.D. Degrees						*M.A. Degrees*					
		Faculty of Pure Science		*Faculty of Political Science*		*Faculty of Philosophy*		*Faculty of Pure Science*		*Faculty of Political Science*		*Faculty of Philosophy*	
Institution	*Total students surveyed*	*1940–45*	*1946–50*	*1940–45*	*1946–50*	*1940–45*	*1946–50*	*1940–45*	*1946–50*	*1940–45*	*1946–50*	*1940–45*	*1946–50*
Columbia College	1,230	29	34	19	10	24	13	29	38	31	42	35	51
Hunter College, New York	1,065	7	10	3	7	3	3	35	48	29	23	22	31
College of the City of New York	1,407	27	33	10	7	17	9	20	30	33	43	27	26
Brooklyn College	1,048	11	27	5	5	6	3	32	44	36	37	29	37
Other New York institutions [a]	1,784	15	16	2	4	3	4	18	41	27	34	28	38
New England institutions [b]	1,548	19	28	10	10	9	4	25	30	30	42	22	48
Southern institutions	1,325	11	18	3	10	11	8	29	31	18	30	19	36
Western institutions [c]	3,258	19	27	12	13	5	6	24	32	24	34	19	41
Foreign institutions	1,865	30	26	14	6	17	18	18	21	21	34	22	25
Pennsylvania institutions [d]	920	18	24	8	6	8	5	23	32	28	38	30	39

[a] Except the above four and except Columbia undergraduate colleges, Barnard College, New York University, Queens College, Fordham University, Yeshiva University, the United States Military Academy, Vassar College, and Cornell University.

[b] Except Harvard, Yale, Wellesley, Smith, and Dartmouth.

[c] Except the Universities of Chicago, Michigan, Wisconsin, and California.

[d] Except Swarthmore College and the University of Pennsylvania.

Note: See Table 52 for figures on institutions excluded here.

tween 1940 and 1956, 34 percent had earned master's degrees by 1956, and 8.6 percent Ph.D.'s (again discounting the 126 Ph.D.'s earned by the group entering after 1950, which would bring the percentage up to a little over 9.) Of the 16,928 students in the same group who had graduated from colleges which were on the now discontinued list of undergraduate colleges approved by the Association of Graduate Schools in the Association of American Universities, 31 percent had earned master's degrees, and 8 percent Ph.D.'s. Of the 15,627 students in the same group who had graduated from colleges with Phi Beta Kappa chapters, 32 percent had earned master's degrees and 8.5 percent Ph.D.'s.

Of the 9,971 students who had graduated from private colleges that had received Ford grants in 1955–56, 33 percent had earned master's degrees, and 8 percent Ph.D.'s. The 1,491 graduates of colleges which had received a Ford grant as well as an accomplishment grant, 32 percent had earned master's degrees, and 8 percent Ph.D.'s. Knapp and Greenbaum's qualitative study of the collegiate origins of the younger American scholar rated Swarthmore, Reed, Chicago, Oberlin, and Haverford at the top of a list of 50 outstanding colleges:[5] 519 graduates from these five colleges entered the Columbia Graduate Faculties between 1940 and 1956, and 36 percent had obtained M.A.'s by 1956, and 10 percent Ph.D.'s. The lowest five on the list of fifty, Monmouth, Kalamazoo, Pennsylvania, Dartmouth and Coe sent 316 graduates, 31 percent of whom earned Master's, and 13 percent of whom earned doctor's degrees.

Since the Graduate Faculties offer special fellowships for graduates from Iowa colleges, the record made by the 203 students from Iowa colleges is interesting: 14 percent earned doctorates, and 33 percent M.A.'s. This record is impressive when we compare it with averages for other states in the Midwest which tend to be a little below the success ratio of about 9 percent Ph.D.'s for the total population surveyed.

Table 3 lists only those few institutions—or groups of institutions—which sent large contingents, about a thousand or more during 1940–50, to Columbia. Students who obtained both the M.A. and Ph.D. degrees were counted only once, among the Ph.D.'s, so that by adding percents for Ph.D.'s and M.A.'s we can establish how large a percentage received any degree. This is an important consideration, for many candidates, especially women, entered the Graduate Faculties with the sole objective of earning a master's degree, so that the low Ph.D. rate of Hunter or Brooklyn graduates, for example, need not be interpreted as a high rate of failure.

Table 4 refers to students born abroad who entered the Graduate Faculties between 1940 and 1951.

Table 4. NUMBER OF FOREIGN-BORN STUDENTS ENTERING COLUMBIA GRADUATE FACULTIES 1940–51 AND PERCENT WITH PH.D. BY 1956

Country	*Number entering 1940–51*	*Percent with Ph.D. by 1956*
	PURE SCIENCE	
Canada	45	47 *
Germany	107	28
Italy	17	24 *
India	43	19 *
England	19	16 *
South America	32	16 *
France	20	10 *
	POLITICAL SCIENCE	
Germany	174	13
England	44	11 *
South America	56	7
Canada	113	6
Italy	32	6 *
India	69	6
	PHILOSOPHY	
Germany	148	20
Canada	79	13
France	51	12
Italy	83	6
South America	61	5
England	39	5 *

* Percentage based on a group smaller than 50.

Like all leading graduate schools, Columbia's Graduate Faculties wish to maintain a national and international representation. Fears have been expressed that the growth of graduate schools in the Midwest and West will threaten the Eastern schools' national following. For the years covered by the detailed study of one Eastern institution, Columbia, no basis for this fear can be found. 33 percent of the total surveyed population of over 23,000 students entering between 1940 and 1956 had graduated from colleges and universities in the New York Metropolitan area and another 10 percent from institutions in New York state. The remaining 57 percent were distributed as follows:

Middle Atlantic states	11 percent
New England	12 percent
South	6 percent
Midwest and West	19 percent
Foreign countries	9 percent

Table 5. ENTERING CLASSES BY COLLEGES OF ORIGIN, 1940–56

Institution	*Total entering 1940–56*	*Percent entering 1940–45*	*Percent entering 1946–50*	*Percent entering 1951–56*
Percent of total population surveyed	100	26	44	30
Columbia College	1,172	18	52	30
Columbia University School of General Studies	612	5	37	58
Barnard College	598	36	34	29
Hunter College	1,010	50	28	22
College of the City of New York	1,344	26	48	26
New York University	767	31	42	26
Brooklyn College	1,001	31	43	26
Queens College, New York	319	24	42	34
Fordham University	213	22	50	28
Yeshiva University	151	34	25	40
United States Military Academy	172	16	38	46
Vassar College	217	35	38	27
Cornell	262	20	42	38
Other institutions in New York state	1,739	29	40	31
Princeton University	183	16	49	34
Rutgers University	208	12	54	34
Other institutions in New Jersey, Delaware, District of Columbia	885	28	47	25
Swarthmore	127	16	49	35
University of Pennsylvania	134	27	45	28
Other Pennsylvania institutions	890	24	47	29
Harvard	425	17	52	31
Yale	267	10	56	34
Wellesley	168	37	29	34
Smith	204	35	37	28
Dartmouth	156	16	53	31
Other New England institutions	1,508	23	45	31
Southern institutions	1,297	25	48	27
University of Chicago	180	30	39	31
University of Michigan	214	21	44	34
University of Wisconsin	156	28	46	26
University of California	293	25	46	29
Other Western and Midwestern institutions	3,170	25	45	30
Foreign institutions	1,810	20	45	35

These percentages remained practically the same in the three periods 1940–45, 1946–50, and 1951–56; there was a slight actual increase of one or two percent in the share of the metropolitan element, and the Midwest and West and South sent a slightly smaller relative contingent toward the end of the period surveyed, but this loss was compensated for by a rise toward the end of the period in the foreign student's share. A slightly larger number of veterans entering after 1945 were graduates of Metropolitan colleges than were the rest of the students. The G.I. Bill evidently encouraged local students who might otherwise not have gone to graduate school.

While the relative contributions of colleges varied in three time intervals, the contributions of various areas of birth were quite stable. A few inferences can be drawn from Table 6. 1. The Graduate Faculties before 1940 attracted slightly larger shares of students not born in New York City than after 1940. 2. The share of foreign students rose steadily over the years. 3. The drop in New York City born entering after 1945 may be due to the general movement to the suburbs—the New York City percentage went down 5 points, and the category which includes the suburbs rose 4 percent.

Table 6. PERCENT OF TOTAL COLUMBIA UNIVERSITY POPULATION ENTERING FACULTY OF POLITICAL SCIENCE

	10 percent sample before 1940	*1940–45*	*1946–48*	*1949–51*	*1952–56*
Total	713	2,149	2,459	2,119	2,084
Born in New York City	30	36	31	31	31
Born in New England and Middle Atlantic states	23	23	27	25	23
Born in Southern and Western states	27	21	21	22	21
Born abroad	19	21	21	22	26

Since the distribution of graduates from a given college is influenced largely by individual professors, it can not be treated statistically. However, definite patterns can be found when we compare students born in certain regions. New York City students, for example, were heavily represented in all sciences except geology, and hardly at all in religion. Students born in the South were strongly represented in religion, English, and Greek and Latin, and students born in the Midwest and West in geology, and music, but relatively little in foreign language departments and mathematics. Foreign-born students made up relatively large shares of foreign language departments, but were represented only in small numbers in English, psychology, music, history, and zoology.

Table 53 affords an overview of relative performances, by years and faculties, of students classified by four main regions of birth. We see, for example, that the performance of students born in New York City was relatively poor in Pure Science but strikingly successful in Political Science; that, roughly speaking, they tended to earn a larger proportion of master's degrees while students born in the South, Midwest, and West earned a larger share of doctorates. Every year a goodly number of students from New York City—frequently secondary school teachers attending in the afternoons and evenings—entered the Graduate Faculties with the primary goal of earning master's degrees. Were it not for the convenient location of Columbia, many of these students would go elsewhere, and in fact they have, in the years since the war, tended to seek master's degrees in other metropolitan institutions. Table 53 clearly shows this trend.

Howard E. Tempero's study of the geographic origins of graduate students established that every graduate school, even the large and influential ones, "obtained a large percentage of its students from a relatively small area propinquent to the university." [6] His conclusion—that certain areas of the country needed to build graduate schools in order to enable larger percentages of their college graduates to enter graduate schools—may be questioned by those who believe that an area or a state builds graduate schools if its citizens show a desire to support such a venture.

Chapter Three. REGISTRATION AND AGE PATTERNS

REGISTRATION PATTERNS

UNLIKE some other graduate schools, Columbia's Graduate Faculties have not up to now required that candidates for graduate degrees carry a full program of courses. Accordingly, unless individual departments prescribe or urge otherwise, students may register for as few or as many courses as they wish. The minimum requirement for an M.A. degree is 30, for a Ph.D. degree 60 points (semester hours). The majority of graduate courses afford 3 points of credit a semester, and a graduate student's full program normally consists of four or five courses—12 or 15 points—so that a master's degree can be earned in one academic year. A doctor's degree could be earned in two years, if no time were needed for the writing of the dissertation. Since up to 9 points can be taken in a summer session, a master's degree can be earned within one calendar year even with a program of 12 points a semester. Hence 12 points, or four courses, may still be considered a full program. It is convenient in later parts of this chapter to distinguish between students who took 10 points or more and those who took 9 points or less. Since the large majority of programs may be expressed in multiples of three, the first group includes mainly those who took programs of *12* or more points. Roughly speaking, the method of division separates full-time from part-time students. Before going into a description of registration patterns between 1940 and 1956, a detailed account of students registered in the academic year 1955–56 may be helpful.

PATTERN OF STUDENT POPULATION 1955–56

Of the 2,629 students who were registered during the academic year 1955–56 and who had begun their studies at Columbia in a fall semester, 1,484 or 56 percent had started their careers in the Graduate Faculties by registering for 13 or more points in their first semester, usually for the normal full program of 15 points consisting generally of five courses, each meeting for a total of a hundred minutes a week.

These "full starters" followed a great variety of registration patterns in later semesters. Some dropped out after their first semester of full work and returned later, sometimes after many years. Others continued steadily but registered for reduced programs. While there were a large number of individual variations of registration patterns, one fact stood out: many "full starters" continued for at least the second semester in a full program. A total of 1,205, or 81 percent of all those who had started in the fall with a program of 13 points or more, continued with 13 points or more for at least the next semester. Another 170, or 11 percent of the entire group of "full starters," continued for the second semester with a program of at least 10 points. *Thus a total of 92 percent of those who started with 13 points or more continued in their second semester with what may be called a full program.*

Of the 109 who after a first full semester dropped to less than 10 points or stayed away entirely, some returned to a full program —6 after more than three years of complete absence. One of those, after an absence of five semesters, eventually completed his Ph.D. degree in history a full twelve years after his first registration. Twenty-three of the students who started out on a full program in September, 1955, had not returned by the end of Summer Session in 1956, and after that date no information for the study was gathered.

Aside from these 23, another 27 "full starters" who had entered the Graduate Faculties prior to September, 1955, did not return for the second semester but returned later for at least a few points. Thus a total of 48 out of a group of 1,484, or only 3 percent of the "full starters," failed to return for the next semester. Compare this low proportion with the percentages for the groups which had started with less than a full program of 13 or more points: of the 374 students who began their first semester taking between 10 and 13 points, over 5 percent did not return for the second semester; of the 278 who started with between 7 and 9 points in their first semester, over 7 percent did not return for the second semester. In the group of 321 starting with between 4 and 6 points, almost 8 percent did not return for the second semester. And of the 172 who started taking less than 4 points in their first semester, 22 percent did not return for the second semester.

Table 7 compares what happened after the first year to the group which took two full semesters and to the group with a slightly reduced second semester.

Table 7. COMPARISON OF STUDENTS TAKING FULL PROGRAM FOR TWO SEMESTERS AND THOSE TAKING REDUCED PROGRAM IN SECOND SEMESTER

	1,205 taking two consecutive semesters of over 13 points (percent)	*170 reducing program from 13 points or over to 10–13 points in second semester (percent)*
Stayed away a full year or more	11	10
Returned for at least a second year of 2 full semesters	13	7.6
Took 10–13 points in 3d semester	10	47
Took 6–9 points in 3d semester	5	15
Took 3–5 points in 3d semester	5	10
Took 3 or less points in 3d semester	4	8

The following registration patterns over the four initial semesters occurred most frequently:

I. 155 students took full programs for four consecutive semesters

II. 137 students took two full semesters, and then did not register at all for two consecutive semesters

III. 64 took a full program for three semesters, and then reduced their loads slightly to between 9 and 12 points in their fourth semester

IV. 54 students carried full programs in their first two semesters, and then took slightly reduced programs (9 to 12 points) in their next two semesters

V. 20 students had full programs in their first, second, and fourth semesters, and a slightly reduced program in their third semester.

The combined patterns I, III, IV, and V form a hard-core group of 293 two-year full-time students. In the total group of 997 "full starters" who by the time the study was undertaken could have completed four semesters, this hard core made up 29 percent.

Among the 1,205 "full starters" who continued in their second semester with a full program, 490, or 40 percent, earned M.A. degrees; 42, or 3.5 percent, earned Ph.D.'s; and 71, or 6 percent, earned both degrees.

Among the 170 "full starters" who in their second semester took a slightly reduced full load of between 9 and 12 points, 52, or 30 percent, earned an M.A. degree; 3, or under 2 percent, earned a Ph.D.; and 8, or 5 percent, earned both degrees.

Among the 109 "full starters" who in their second semester reduced their program to less than 10 points, 25, or 23 percent, earned an M.A. degree; 4, or 4 percent, earned a Ph.D.; and two earned both degrees.

Of the entire population, 374, or 14 percent, started with between 10 and 12 points in their first semester. Of this group, 46 percent continued with an equally heavy program, another 29 percent increased their program to 13 points or over, and another 11 percent reduced their loads slightly. Altogether, 84 percent in their second semesters stayed close to their first semester pattern.

Those who started with between 7 and 9 points numbered 278, or 10 percent of the entire population. Of these 278, 39 percent continued with a program identical with the first semester's program, another 17 percent increased their second semester's program slightly, and another 20 percent reduced it slightly, so that altogether 76 percent stayed close to their first semester's pattern.

Three hundred and nineteen, or 12 percent, started with between 3 and 6 points, and altogether 82 percent of this group followed a similar or identical pattern in the second semester.

Three or less points were taken in the beginning programs of 172, or 7 percent, of the population. Of this group 70 percent continued for an identical or similar program in the second semester.

By far the largest percentage continuing for a second semester with an identical point load was in the group taking more than 13 points—81 percent. All other groups—those starting with 1 to 3, 4 to 6, 7 to 9, or 10 to 12 points—had considerably smaller percentages continuing with identical point loads: 47, 46, 39, and 46 percent respectively.

Our analysis of the student population registered in 1955–56 established the fact that all students tend to follow a pattern of heavy or light registration generally as established in their first semester. We can also state that more students who carry heavier programs are consistent in maintaining their pattern of registration than are those students who carry relatively lighter programs.

STUDENT REGISTRATION PATTERNS BY DEPARTMENTS, 1940–51

As we saw in the preceding paragraphs, many students tended to continue in their second semester with a program of courses equally or similarly concentrated as in the first semester. Table 8

Table 8. REGISTRATION PATTERNS BY DEPARTMENTS, 1940–51

Department	*Percent of students carrying 10 points or more in first semester who carried 10 points or more in second semester*	*Percent of department total carrying 10 or more points in first and second semesters*
	PURE SCIENCE	
Chemistry	77	55
Geology	88	64
Mathematics	80	37
Psychology	78	46
Physics	84	55
Zoology	72	48
	POLITICAL SCIENCE	
Anthropology	82	56
Economics	83	51
History	79	49
Mathematical Statistics	81	49
Public Law	78	54
Sociology	77	45
	PHILOSOPHY	
English	82	54
Fine Arts	75	40
French	75	44
Music	74	30
Philosophy	77	49
Religion	84	59
Spanish	78	31

Table 9. REGISTRATION PATTERNS OF STUDENTS DISCONTINUING IN SECOND SEMESTER

Department	*Students taking 9 points or less in first semester*		*Students taking at least 10 points in first semester*	
	Percent	*Number*	*Percent*	*Number*
	PURE SCIENCE			
Chemistry	40	78	9	46
Geology	34	29	5	12
Mathematics	26	90	6	20
Psychology	49	119	7	26
Physics	34	67	6	26
Zoology	29	25	15	26
	POLITICAL SCIENCE			
Anthropology	38	45	8	20
Economics	39	234	7	77
History	25	174	7	83
Mathematical Statistics	37	37	7	12
Public Law	33	145	10	110
Sociology	33	134	8	48
	PHILOSOPHY			
English	26	297	8	200
French	28	63	7	26
Philosophy	29	65	11	45
Religion	18	16	3	6
Spanish	26	79	10	23

shows the slight variations among departments for students starting in 1940–51, but it confirms the findings made for the group registered in 1955 to 1956, that students who start full time tend to continue full time for at least another semester.

Relatively few of those students who began with a program of at least 10 points left after one semester: from 15 percent in Zoology down to a percentage of 4 or less in Greek and Latin, Religion, Italian, and Engineering. By far the largest number of those who began with a reduced program of 9 or less points continued taking a light program, from 80 percent in Greek and Latin to 47 percent in Chemistry, 64 percent in English, and 34 percent in Geology. Whereas only between 15 and 1 percent of those who began with 10 or more points left the University during or after the first semester, larger proportions of those who began with 9 or less points did, for example, 40 percent in Chemistry and 26 percent in English (see Table 9).

Some departments, especially in the sciences, discourage part-time students both in their admissions policy and by offering few or no courses in the late afternoons and evenings, while others such as Spanish offer most of their courses after working hours. The relative proportions in given departments of students carrying 10 or more points for at least their first two semesters vary from 64 to 31 percent. Since many graduate schools are curious to know to what extent students who begin with a reduced program leave after only one semester, Table 9, listing students entering seventeen large departments 1940–56 is of especial interest.

Students who began with a program of 10 or more points and dropped to a program of 9 or less points in their second semester made up a relatively small part of *all* students; 11 percent in German and French, 10 percent in Chemistry, 8 percent in History, 7 percent in English, and 5 percent in geology. An even smaller percentage stepped up a program of 9 or less points in the first semester to 10 or more in the second: 9 percent in Geology, 3 percent in Chemistry, 4 percent in History, 3 percent in English, and 1 percent in Mathematical Statistics.

A sample of students who entered before 1940 contained lower proportions of students taking 10 points or more for at least two semesters than did groups entering later.

Table 10. PERCENT OF ENTERING CLASSES TAKING AT LEAST 10 POINTS FOR AT LEAST TWO SEMESTERS

Faculty	*Before 1940*	*1940–42*	*1943–45*	*1946–48*	*1949–51*	*1952–56*
Pure Science	32	34	27	59	57	51
Political Science	30	30	30	62	58	45
Philosophy	28	31	29	59	56	43

At the opposite extreme are those students who disappeared after one semester of 9 points or less. Note the influence of the war years.

Table 11. PERCENT OF ENTERING CLASSES TAKING 9 POINTS OR LESS AND DISCONTINUING IN SECOND SEMESTER

Faculty	*Before 1940*	*1940–42*	*1943–45*	*1946–48*	*1949–51*	*1952–56* *
Pure Science	12	21	21	7	6	9
Political Science	13	19	21	7	7	13
Philosophy	14	17	16	7	6	10

* Figures for 1952–56 are distorted because they include those starting in February, 1956, who by the end of the study could not possibly have taken more than one semester.

The conclusion is justified that in the 16 year span studied there was a trend toward beginning graduate study with more concentrated programs. Among those who eventually earned a Ph.D. degree many lightened their loads as they advanced in graduate school, but only relatively few of those who never registered for a full-time semester earned doctor's degrees. Of the 151 Ph.D.'s in English earned by those who entered between 1940 and 1956, only 18 had never registered for a full semester; there were 14 out of 84 in French, 3 out of 25 in Spanish, and 5 out of 89 in philosophy; 7 out of 121 Ph.D.'s in physics; 6 out of 26 in mathematics, but only 13 out of 251 in chemistry, were earned by students who had never carried a full-time program; and 12 out of 185 Ph.D.'s in history, 6 out of 103 in public law and government, 7 out of 119 in economics, and 4 out of 61 in sociology had never registered for a full program.

Between 13 and 16 percent of *all* students—irrespective of their course load—entering between 1940 and 1956 left the university after only one semester (or entered one semester before the end of the census), and between 18 and 27 percent after two; between 28 and 38 percent stayed for between three and six semesters, and between 22 and 32 percent for seven and more semesters. Since the entire population surveyed consisted partly of classes which could have stayed only a limited number of semesters, by the end of the survey in July 1956, a count such as this exaggerates the share of students staying only a short span. None of the 1,257 students entering in 1955, for example, could possibly have taken more than three semesters by the time the survey was made, and they make up about 5 percent of the entire group on which the percentages are based.

New York City students accounted consistently for a slightly larger share of those who stayed one semester only, and also of those who stayed seven semesters and more.

Table 12 shows how few students managed to earn master's degrees in the minimum time of two semesters. The departments of Music and Fine Arts ask candidates for the master's degrees to spread their thirty points of registration over at least four (rather than the standard two) semesters.

Table 12. STUDENTS ENTERING 1940–56 AND EARNING M.A. BY 1956 (*In percent*)

Department	*Total without Ph.D. earning M.A. by 1956*	*Total earning M.A. and taking 10 or more points for 2 semesters*	*3 semesters*
	PURE SCIENCE		
Chemistry	39	35	9
Geology	44	25	8
Mathematics	39	24	2
Physics	28	12	8
Psychology	49	54	2
Zoology	38	27	2
	POLITICAL SCIENCE		
Economics	25	31	4
History	39	25	3
Public Law	33	28	2
Sociology	24	24	3
	PHILOSOPHY		
English	37	37	3
Fine Arts	25	12	1
French	28	22	2
Music	38	5	1
Philosophy	22	18	3
Religion	13	13	4
Spanish	25	26	2

Students who consistently registered for part-time programs are shown to have had poorer chances of earning degrees than others. In zoology, for example, only 4 percent of those who had earned master's degrees were part-time students in all their semesters, but of those who received no degree at all 15 percent had been part-time students throughout.

Students who were not successful in earning degrees and who in no semester carried a program of more than 9 points were also inclined to leave after only two semesters. More than half of the unsuccessful candidates who took only 9 points or less per semester left after only one or two semesters. In other words, a good number of the unsuccessful candidates simply dropped out of graduate school before they had taken enough credits for a degree.

On the other hand, as Table 14 shows, sizable percentages of those who never received any degrees had been full-time students for at least two semesters. It is not possible to suggest reasons for the variations among departments, such as relatively more stringent degree requirements. Among the departments in which those taking at least two full programs failed relatively frequently were some that award master's degrees as terminal awards to students who are not permitted to continue toward a Ph.D. and others that require the passing of difficult and very comprehensive masters' examinations. A low rate of failure obviously can be caused by careful screening in the first semester, or else by making the master's degree easy.

The three main groups, nonveteran men, veterans, and women students differed markedly in the manner in which they began their studies, and the differences were also marked according to the year of entrance.

Only 44 percent of the men not veterans who entered in 1940 began with a course load of 10 or more points. In the war years even fewer men students began with full programs, and in 1943 only 23 percent of the men began with a program of 10 points or

Table 13. STUDENTS ENTERING 1940–56, EARNING M.A. BY 1956, AND TAKING NO MORE THAN 9 POINTS IN ANY SEMESTER

Department	*Number of students surveyed*	*Percent earning M.A. by 1956*	*Percent earning M.A. and taking no more than 9 points in any semester*	*Percent with no degree taking no more than 9 points in any semester*
		PURE SCIENCE		
Chemistry	684	39	5	13
Geology	320	44	9	10
Mathematics	827	39	14	30
Physics	744	28	8	13
Psychology	663	49	11	20
Zoology	274	38	4	15
		POLITICAL SCIENCE		
Economics	1,857	35	8	20
History	2,459	39	13	28
Public Law	2,084	33	8	21
Sociology	1,208	24	15	25
		PHILOSOPHY		
English	4,574	37	9	23
Fine Arts	268	25	15	21
French	704	28	14	25
Music	260	38	25	39
Philosophy	763	22	9	23
Religion	379	16	13	20
Spanish	606	25	21	39

more. After the war the number of men registering for 10 and more points rose rapidly to a high of 77 percent in 1952.

Veterans entering after the war tended even more than non-veterans to begin with programs of 10 and more points: 83 percent of all veterans entering in 1948 carried such a program. Veterans entering after 1950 took relatively lighter programs than the non-veterans—only 55 percent in 1952 as against 77 percent of the non-veterans. A possible explanation for this is given on page 66.

Table 14. STUDENTS WITH NO DEGREE BY 1956 TAKING 10 OR MORE POINTS FOR AT LEAST TWO SEMESTERS

Department	*Percent*
PURE SCIENCE	
Chemistry	26
Geology	28
Mathematics	12
Physics	32
Psychology	9
Zoology	21
POLITICAL SCIENCE	
Economics	24
History	18
Public Law	25
Sociology	21
PHILOSOPHY	
English	24
Fine Arts	17
French	17
Music	9
Philosophy	18
Religion	23
Spanish	11

Of the women starting in 1940, 43 percent carried 10 or more points, and as relatively more women entered in the war years, the percentage of those who started with full programs went down, reaching a low of 30 in 1943; that was also the low point for men. In the years after the war between 50 and 60 percent of the women began their studies with a program of 10 or more points.

As could be expected, students who began with a program of 10 or more points were apt to complete enough points for at least a master's degree, and large numbers accumulated 40 points of credit and more. Conversely, relatively small numbers of those who began with a full program completed fewer points than needed for at least a master's degree. Table 15 demonstrates to what extent the program in a student's first semester and his chances of completing at least a master's program were related. To illustrate the table: 25 percent of nonveteran men entering in 1940 who in their first semester took 10 points or more had completed less than 30 points by July, 1956.

Irrespective of their geographic origin or the Faculty in which

Table 15. FIRST SEMESTER PROGRAMS OF STUDENTS ENTERING 1940–54 AND COMPLETING LESS THAN 30 POINTS BY JULY, 1956 (*Percents of defined groups*)

	Nonveteran Men		*Veterans*		*Women*	
Year of entrance	*10 points or more*	*9 points or less*	*10 points or more*	*9 points or less*	*10 points or more*	*9 points or less*
1940	25	76	6 *	23 *	19	76
1941	41	80	6 *	19 *	20	80
1942	37	73	29 *	36 *	23	77
1943	26	70	0 *	38 *	24	70
1944	27	71	7 *	41 *	17	74
1945	22	70	21	50 *	24	69
1946	17	70	18	59	15	68
1947	17	62	12	57	17	63
1948	22	63	11	66	21	69
1949	19	74	13	57	23	64
1950	26	72	14	68	21	64
1951	25	70	25	62	22	71
1952	25	77	35	82	21	75
1953	31	81	31	87	28	84
1954	38	94	41 *	0 *	50	97

* Percentage based on a group smaller than 50.

they registered, between 48 and 64 percent of all students surveyed began their graduate studies with at least two full semesters. Those who began with a full-time semester and dropped to part-time registration in their second semester accounted for between 8 and 11 percent, those who began with a part-time semester and continued full time in their second semester for between 3 and 9 percent, and those who began with two part-time semesters for between 21 and 36 percent. Generally, fewer part-time students were in science than in political science and philosophy. This was to be expected, as was the fact that New York City students were more likely to attend part time than were students from New

England. Similarly, those from the Middle Atlantic states were less frequently full-time students than were the students from Southern, Midwestern, and Western states, though the differences were small.

Table 16, arranged by Faculties and by the three groups of nonveteran men students, Second World War veterans, and women students, lists students entering 1940–56 by the manner in which they registered in their first two semesters. Category I began with two full semesters (10 points or more); Category II with one full, one part-time (9 points or less) semester; Category III began with a part-time semester but carried a full program in the second semester; Category IV began with two part-time semesters. After the total numbers of students in each category, both the actual numbers of Ph.D.'s earned and the percent of the total which the Ph.D.'s represent are listed. Of the 1,597 nonveteran men who entered the Faculty of Pure Science between 1940 and 1956 and who began their studies with two full-time semesters, 484 individuals, or 30 percent earned a Ph.D.

The evidence in favor of starting full-time presented here and in Table 55 is clear. With two exceptions—the M.A.'s in geology and the Ph.D.'s in music—students who began with two full-time semesters were more successful in earning graduate degrees than students who began with two part-time semesters. The entire geology group of part-time students consisted of 29 and therefore may safely be ignored. The Music Department, which advises all its students to register only for part-time programs, awarded only a total of seven Ph.D.'s in the entire period surveyed, and may also be ignored.

Those students who took a full program in their first semester but dropped to a reduced program in their second semester performed more nearly as the students who took two full semesters than those who began with two reduced semesters. However, those relatively few students—generally 5 or less percent of all students—whose first semester was part time and whose second semester full time, often performed better than those who began with two full-time semesters. Quite possibly the students who stepped up their programs in the second semester were February starters who began with a light program simply because certain full-year courses

Table 16. STUDENTS ENTERING 1940–56 AND EARNING PH.D. BY 1956, BY REGISTRATION CATEGORIES

Faculty	*Category*	*Total*	*Ph.D.'s awarded*	*Percent*
		NONVETERAN MEN		
Pure Science	I	1,597	484	30
	II	264	66	25
	III	171	60	35
	IV	817	140	17
Political Science	I	2,042	332	16
	II	370	46	12
	III	138	25	18
	IV	1,051	91	9
Philosophy	I	1,480	213	14
	II	275	33	12
	III	127	21	17
	IV	863	106	12
		SECOND WORLD WAR VETERANS		
Pure Science	I	836	282	34
	II	112	26	23
	III	78	23	29
	IV	236	37	16
Political Science	I	1,803	257	14
	II	223	16	7
	III	68	3	4
	IV	459	28	6
Philosophy	I	1,498	178	12
	II	171	12	7
	III	66	3	5
	IV	368	26	7
		WOMEN		
Pure Science	I	650	125	19
	II	141	17	12
	III	87	19	22
	IV	579	44	8
Political Science	I	1,209	101	8
	II	261	13	5
	III	132	9	7
	IV	1,106	31	3
Philosophy	I	1,721	112	7
	II	383	14	4
	III	181	9	5
	IV	1,696	51	3

were closed to them; February starters as a group may be slightly better in their performance because among them are bright and ambitious college students who finished a semester early and others who for one reason or another are so anxious to get started that they do not wait until the traditional September date. It is also possible that among Columbia's February starters were students who had applied to more selective graduate schools that do not accept new students in February.

What conclusions may be drawn from what has been so far said about registration patterns? Clearly, the pattern set in the first semester tended to prevail in later semesters. Clearly, those students who began their studies with a full load of courses tended to complete more points than those who began with a lighter load, and were more apt to succeed in getting a degree than those who began part-time. Those with unquestioning faith in averages will conclude that all graduate students should be made to register for full programs.

But one can make two reasonable statements relevant to the issue: 1. Students who begin full time have a better chance of success. 2. Students who have certain traits or advantages—enough money to attend full time, high motivation, confidence in themselves, and a high rating in college—are also likely to succeed. These traits will influence the decision to begin with a full program, whereas the marginal candidates may tend to start with lighter loads. A light program may not only be a *cause,* but also a *symptom.*

While statistically it may appear that part-time students are less successful than full-time students, it would be unfair to argue that all are indifferent or half-hearted about their studies; many individual part-time students have been successful beyond the average. The problems of the part-time graduate student are, however, complex and at present too little investigated to be taken up in this necessarily limited study.

Every year a certain number of students who have done graduate work before at another university enter the Graduate Faculties. Others, after attending Columbia's graduate school for some time, go to another graduate school, and finally return to Columbia. If graduate work taken elsewhere has bearing on graduate studies at Columbia, credit toward the Columbia doctor's degree is given for it. This credit is called advanced standing. Table 17 gives some idea of the extent to which over the years students have come to Columbia from other graduate schools, but it does not tell the full story of transfer students, for those who attended another university without receiving credit are omitted from the survey. The largest share of students with credit from other graduate schools was in the group entering the Faculty of Pure Science in the years after the war, a somewhat older group with a large percentage of veterans. Relatively fewer students in the Faculty of Philosophy came from other universities, and slightly more in Pure Science

Table 17. STUDENTS ENTERING WITH ADVANCED STANDING, 1940–51 (*In percent*)

Year of entrance	*Total number of students*	*Percent with advanced standing*
	PURE SCIENCE	
Before 1940 *	636	8
1940–42	762	11
1943–45	769	7
1946–48	1,372	14
1949–51	1,139	11
	POLITICAL SCIENCE	
Before 1940 *	727	11
1940–42	999	12
1943–45	1,175	10
1946–48	2,500	11
1949–51	2,146	10
	PHILOSOPHY	
Before 1940 *	887	8
1940–42	991	10
1943–45	1,255	7
1946–48	2,252	8
1949–51	2,212	7

* Figures based on a 10 percent sample.

than in Political Science. The relative differences were slight, 7 being lowest, and 14 the highest percentage of students with credit from other graduate schools in any of the groups tabulated.

AGE PATTERNS

The twenty-four thousand students, roughly, who entered Columbia University's Graduate Faculties between 1940 and 1956 may be divided into six groups according to their age at entrance:

1. Very young students, those aged 20 and under, primarily twenty-year-olds who entered college young and finished in less than average time, an unusually talented group. 2. The group of students 21–22 years old who completed college on schedule and proceeded into graduate school without any delay. 3. A group 23–25 years old, who may have graduated with a slight delay or who may have interrupted their studies between college and graduate school, either to serve a short term in the army, to try their hand on a job, to earn some money, or perhaps to try a professional school. 4. Those entering between the ages of 26 and 29, usually veterans with extended army duty and others similar to those in the preceding age group. 5. Students entering between the ages of 30 and 49, a group accounting for less than one-fifth of the entire population here described, and which is interesting because it is widely diversified in background: secondary school teachers who want to become college teachers, married women whose children have grown up, foreign students and immigrants. 6. The sixth group, which never contributes more than 2 percent of the entire student population, is made up of those who enter the Graduate Faculties at the age of 50 and over.

Relatively more young students enter the science departments than the humanities and social sciences. For the entire period from 1940 to 1956, the three faculties accounted for different shares of the groups entering at different ages.

Table 18. VARIOUS AGE GROUPS ENTERING, 1940–56 (*In percent*)

	16–20	*21–22*	*23–25*	*26–29*	*30–49*	*Over 50*
Pure Science	9	29	29	19	15	0.5
Political Science	5	24	28	22	20	0.5
Philosophy	5	26	28	19	20	1.0

Of the students entering the faculties of Pure Science, Political Science, and Philosophy between the years 1940 and 1942, 11, 12, and 7 percent respectively were aged 20 or under. In a sample of 10 percent of students registered before 1940, 13, 5, and 5 percent respectively entered the three faculties at the age of 20 or under. After 1940 the relative size of the classes entering at the age of 20 or under decreased. The efforts of foundations to encourage admission to college of high school sophomores and juniors may be too recent, and possibly on too small a scale, to be noticeable. It is also possible that the relative decrease of young students was caused by a relative increase of older students. Such an increase clearly took place after the second world war, and may have continued due to other causes. For details, see Table 54.

Aside from the relative decrease of the group which entered at a young age, the increase in the groups aged 23 to 29 at entrance during the two periods 1946–51—the veterans' years, so to speak—was most remarkable.

Table 19. AGE GROUPS OF STUDENTS ENTERING 1940–56, BY FACULTY (*In percent*)

		Ages at Entrance					
Years	*Number*	*16–20*	*21–22*	*23–25*	*26–29*	*30–49*	*Over 50*
		PURE SCIENCE					
1940–42	762	11	34	25	14	14	1
1943–45	768	14	32	22	14	16	1
1946–48	1,371	7	19	35	23	13	0
1949–51	1,139	4	25	32	23	13	1
1952–54	807	3	31	29	20	15	0
1955–56	337 *	3	27	27	23	18	1
		POLITICAL SCIENCE					
1940–42	998	12	29	22	15	19	1
1943–45	1,176	9	29	22	16	21	1
1946–48	2,497	4	16	32	27	18	1
1949–51	2,146	2	20	29	24	21	0
1952–54	1,471	2	25	28	21	20	1
1955–56	666 *	2	22	27	23	23	1
		PHILOSOPHY					
1940–42	990	7	29	24	13	24	2
1943–45	1,255	8	31	25	12	20	1
1946–48	2,256	5	20	30	12	20	1
1949–51	2,212	2	23	29	22	20	1
1952–54	1,314	2	30	29	18	16	1
1955–56	573 *	2	25	34	18	17	2

* Partial count.

Those who entered graduate work at certain ages seemed to be more successful in earning Ph.D. degrees than others. In most fields, as we shall see on Table 21, the small group entering at 20 or under had a higher rate of success than the older groups. This is not surprising. Those who entered graduate school very young were often persons who graduated young from high school and who completed their college education in minimum time—in other words, generally students of exceptional intelligence. The pattern of success varies from department to department, of course. In Physics the rate of success decreased slightly with increasing age of entry. In the French department, although the differences were slight, the opposite would seem to be true. The rates of success

Table 20. AGE GROUPS OF STUDENTS ENTERING 1940–51, BY DEPARTMENT (*In percent*)

Department	*Number*	*Ages at Entrance* 16–20	21–22	23–25	26–29	30–49	50 and over
		PURE SCIENCE					
Chemistry	747	12	30	33	15	8	0
Geology	311	4	24	30	27	12	0
Mathematics	706	11	27	27	16	17	1
Psychology	632	11	31	26	15	15	0
Physics	627	7	26	39	18	8	1
Zoology	259	11	36	23	19	9	0
		POLITICAL SCIENCE					
Anthropology	370	5	23	27	22	22	1
Economcis	1,670	6	22	29	22	18	1
History	1,936	5	23	29	21	18	1
Mathematical Statistics	275	7	19	33	21	18	0
Public Law	1,537	5	19	26	25	21	1
Sociology	1,029	5	21	28	21	23	1
		PHILOSOPHY					
English	3,716	5	25	30	21	17	1
Fine Arts	192	4	24	24	21	23	2
French	599	5	26	25	17	23	1
German	132	4	17	29	23	23	1
Greek and Latin	136	7	32	19	18	21	1
Italian	122	2	31	18	23	20	2
Music	198	3	27	27	18	24	1
Non-Indo-European Languages	245	5	13	24	19	36	3
Philosophy	641	3	21	34	22	16	0
Religion	320	1	8	23	27	40	1
Spanish	555	7	31	21	14	23	1
Slavic	177	1	13	20	21	41	2

in earning a Ph.D. degree were fairly close in any given department, irrespective of the age when graduate work was begun, except for the group beginning at the age of 50 or over, where the figures were too small to permit valid statements.

The rates of success in earning Ph.D. degrees in the Chemistry department among the groups arranged by age at entrance varied between 37 and 18 percent; in English between 2 and 5 percent; in History between 6 and 11 percent; in Economics between 6 and 8 percent.

In tabulating the extent to which students who had entered at

Table 21. AGE GROUPS OF STUDENTS EARNING PH.D. BY 1956 (*In percent*)

Department	*Ages at Entrance* 16–20	21–22	23–25	26–29	30–49	50 and over
PURE SCIENCE						
Chemistry	31	36	33	37	18	0 *
Geology	38 *	32	35	33	21 *	0 *
Mathematics	10	3	3	4	1	0
Psychology	19	11	25	24	13	0 *
Physics	33 *	24	21	11	4	0 *
Zoology	18 *	15	23	29 *	21 *	0 *
POLITICAL SCIENCE						
Anthropology	29 *	9	17	21	16	0 *
Economics	7	6	8	7	6	6 *
History	11	6	11	9	11	10 *
Mathematical Statistics	11 *	4	8	9	8	0 *
Public Law	7	5	8	6	6	20 *
Sociology	4	5	4	8	7	0 *
PHILOSOPHY						
English	5	2	4	5	5	0 *
Fine Arts	0 *	4 *	2 *	2 *	9 *	0 *
French	19 *	10	13	14	15	0 *
German	33 *	3 *	0 *	4 *	13 *	30 *
Greek and Latin	10 *	2 *	4 *	8 *	10 *	0 *
Italian	33 *	3 *	0 *	4 *	13 *	30 *
Music	40 *	0 *	2	9 *	2 *	0 *
Non-Indo-European Languages	8 *	6 *	10	20 *	13	0 *
Philosophy	9 *	2	16	12	13	33 *
Religion	50 *	13 *	22	30	26	25 *
Slavic	50 *	4 *	9 *	22 *	11	0 *
Spanish	0 *	4	8	5	3	0 *

* Percentage based on a group smaller than 50.

given ages had succeeded in earning Ph.D. degrees by July 1956, only students who entered between 1940 and 1951 were considered, and those who had also earned M.A.'s were included. (The extent to which Ph.D. candidates also earn master's degrees is listed on Table 44). Note that those figures do not represent the total number of degrees which eventually will be awarded to the students here listed. Those entering in 1951 had only five years to earn a degree, considerably less than the mean for many fields (see Table 56). To illustrate Table 21, of the students who between the years 1940 and 1951 had entered the department of Chemistry at the age

Table 22. AGE GROUP OF STUDENTS EARNING M.A. BY 1956 *(In percent)*

Department	*Ages at Entrance* 16–20	21–22	23–25	26–29	30–49	50 and over
PURE SCIENCE						
Chemistry	36	27	27	21	20	50 *
Geology	38 *	46	29	23	29 *	0 *
Mathematics	57	45	44	31	32	25 *
Psychology	47	55	35	22	33	0 *
Physics	23 *	29	28	28	14	20 *
Zoology	32 *	43	28	27 *	21 *	0 *
POLITICAL SCIENCE						
Anthropology	18 *	14	6	15	13	0
Economics	52	40	34	33	26	25 *
History	51	56	40	33	26	20 *
Mathematical Statistics	42 *	42	36	21	24	0 *
Public Law	44	42	37	28	28	13 *
Sociology	43	27	26	21	20	0 *
PHILOSOPHY						
English	48	44	42	41	23	10 *
Fine Arts	38 *	24 *	32 *	29 *	25 *	0 *
French	26 *	38	23	27	19	20 *
German	67 *	24 *	32 *	36 *	13 *	30 *
Greek and Latin	70 *	42 *	46 *	20 *	38 *	100 *
Italian	67 *	24 *	32 *	36 *	13 *	33 *
Music	20 *	57 *	56	37 *	21 *	0 *
Non-Indo-European Languages	17 *	32 *	36	17 *	9	15 *
Philosophy	32 *	28	20	18	13	33 *
Religion	0 *	33 *	17	9	9	25 *
Slavic	50 *	43 *	49 *	24 *	19	33 *
Spanish	33 *	33	22	25	17	0 *

* Percentage based on a group smaller than 50.

of 20 or under, 31 percent had earned a doctor's degree by July, 1956.

In tabulating the extent to which students entering at given ages had succeeded in earning master's degrees by July, 1956, only students who entered between 1940 and 1951 were considered, and those who earned Ph.D.'s as well were omitted, since they had been counted with the Ph.D. group. To illustrate Table 22, of the students who entered the Chemistry department at the age of 20 or under, 36 percent had earned a master's degree by July, 1956.

The figures for language departments such as Germanic Languages, Italian Greek and Latin, and others not of the Indo-European group, were too small to allow generalizations; but, as in Slavic Languages, students entering at a relatively later age had as good or even better chances of success than younger students. A possible explanation would be that it takes many years to acquire the facility necessary for success in these fields, and that younger students who must acquire language skills while in graduate school are more apt to become discouraged than those who enter at an older age, presumably with some knowledge of the language. As for the relatively high rate of success among graduate students in Religion entering after the age of 25, here many successful candidates typically enter that program with a bachelor of divinity degree, and often even a few years after ordination. Like their colleagues in certain languages, they begin graduate study with a head start.

Only rarely was the group with the highest percent of entrants also the group with the highest percent of successful Ph.D. candidates. Table 23 shows by departments the most numerous of the six groups by age at entrance, and those age groups whose members had been relatively most successful in earning Ph.D. and master's degrees. Only in the departments of Economics, History, Public Law and Government, and Philosophy was the age-at-entrance group with the highest number of students also that with the highest percent of successful Ph.D. candidates.

Since few students under present circumstances are able to enter graduate work by the time they are 20 years old, we should perhaps disregard the high rate of success of this very young group. But, even when we do, the age-at-entrance group with the highest percent of members is generally not identical with that group which has the highest number of Ph.D.'s. Whatever the laws of reward that regulate the natural flow of people toward or away from certain enterprises, they do not seem to operate in the field of graduate study.

One of the proposals made to provide college teachers for the future has been the recruiting of older men and women into college teaching. Retired army and navy officers, it has been suggested, might acquire graduate degrees and become college professors. This suggestion has been coupled with the facetious

Table 23. AGE GROUPS MOST FREQUENT AND MOST SUCCESSFUL IN EARNING PH.D. AND M.A. DEGREES

Department or school	*Most frequent age-at-entrance group*	*Group most successful in earning Ph.D.*	*Group most successful in earning M.A.*
	PURE SCIENCE		
Chemistry	23–25	26–29	16–20
Geology	23–25	16–20	21–22
Mathematics	21–25	16–20	16–20
Medical Science	23–25	26–29	16–20
Physics	23–25	16–20	21–22
Psychology	21–22	23–25	21–22
Zoology	21–22	26–29	21–22
	POLITICAL SCIENCE		
Anthropology	23–25	16–20	16–20
Economics	23–25	23–25	16–20
History	23–25	16–20, 23–25, 30–49	21–22
Mathematical Statistics	23–25	16–20	16–22
Public Law	23–25	23–25	50–79
Sociology	23–25	26–29	16–20
	PHILOSOPHY		
Christian Education	30–49	No Ph.D. offered	21–22
English	23–25	16–20, 26–29, 30–49	16–20
French	21–22	16–20	21–22
German	23–25	26–29	16–20
Greek and Latin	21–22	16–20, 30–49	16–20
Italian	21–22	16–20	16–20
Music	21–25	26–29	21–22
Non-Indo-European Languages	30–49	26–29	23–25
Philosophy	23–25	23–25	16–20
Religion	40–49	26–29	21–22
Slavic	30–49	16–20	16–20
Spanish	21–22	23–25	16–22

observation that only people with an independent income such as a pension can afford to become college teachers. Our figures for students over 50 are small and inconclusive, but they all support an attitude of reserve towards older students. The 9 Ph.D. degrees earned among the 152 students who entered at the age of 50 or over were one each in Engineering, Economics, History, Italian, Philosophy, Religion, and 3 (out of 16 candidates) in Public Law and Government. None of the 33 who entered the English department at the age of 50 or over had earned a degree by the end of our tabulation.

In the years 1940–45, graduates of certain colleges or groups of colleges entered Columbia predominantly when they were 23 or less. For example, 84 percent of the 77 entering Queens College graduates were 23 or under. Other metropolitan colleges had similarly high percentages of young students entering the Graduate Faculties.

Hunter College	76 percent
Brooklyn College	74
Columbia College	67
Barnard College	65

But only 56 percent of New York University's graduates were aged 23 or less, 55 percent of C.C.N.Y.'s, and 37 percent of Fordham's.

Vassar, Smith, and Wellesley graduates entering at 23 or under made up 71, 65, and 61 percent of the total respectively. Graduates from well-known Eastern men's colleges did not tend to enter young to the same extent. The age group 23 and under accounted for 40 percent of Dartmouth's small contingent, 38 percent of Harvard's, 30 percent of Princeton's, and 26 percent of Yale's. These figures are all the more significant when we compare them to Columbia College's 67 percent.

Of graduates from the University of Michigan, 57 percent entered at the age of 23 or under, and from the University of Wisconsin 40 percent. For Chicago the percentage was 31, and for the University of California (all campuses) 34. The other Midwestern and Western colleges and universities accounted for a total of 3,258, of whom 38 percent entered at 23 or under. Of the 1,324 from Southern colleges, 35 percent entered at 23 and under, and only 15 percent of the 1,865 graduates from foreign universities entered at that age.

For the period from 1946 to 1950 the age distribution at entrance shifted generally toward the group between 24 and 29 years of age, due primarily to the veterans' arrival, and accordingly the percentage of students entering at 23 and under decreased. Queens College graduates who entered at the young age level now accounted for only 53 percent of the Queens total, and the figures for young students from other metropolitan colleges too went down. Women's colleges generally maintained the same rate of young entrants. The period 1951–56 showed a slight movement toward the 1940–45 distribution by ages.

It must be remembered that in grouping students by ages other factors may intrude. Very young students, for example, are more likely to be single, to receive money from their parents, to be less preoccupied with financial worries. Older students, on the other hand, may feel more keenly a variety of pressures toward completing a degree. The figures on Table 54 show a relatively higher rate of success for older women, indicating that very young women may be more easily distracted from their studies. In Columbia's population, a disproportionate share of students in their middle and late twenties were veterans, therefore financial support bears on the age categories. It seems obvious that more detailed studies of the relationship between age and success in graduate school are needed.

Chapter Four. FINANCIAL SUPPORT FOR GRADUATE STUDENTS

AN AFRICAN STUDENT in Columbia's department of Public Law and Government consistently failed to produce the kind of work which his teachers, impressed by his great intelligence and other qualities, expected of him. It took a long interview with an understanding dean, the late Edgar G. Miller, Jr., to establish the fact that the support which the student received from an outside source fell short by 150 dollars of balancing his extremely modest budget. "We think it is a sound policy," the donor of the fellowship explained, "to give applicants a little less than they need. It is good for their self-reliance to contribute at least a small sum from their own earnings toward their support." After another long talk the dean decided to close the gap in the student's budget by a small grant-in-aid, and almost immediately his grades began to improve.

The story illustrates how difficult it is to generalize about financial support. What may be wise for certain American students did not apply to the student from Africa. It took him countless hours of waiting in employment offices, obtaining from the Immigration Service special permissions to work, and many more hours of worry and uncertainty in a situation which was fundamentally less secure than that of an American student. Conceivably, the fact that his fellowship was not quite adequate destroyed the self-reliance and *amour propre* which the well-meaning donor had hoped to strengthen.

Dean Peter Elder of Harvard's graduate school, recommended in his 1958 report that self-confidence among graduate students be encouraged: "Constant examinations, constant judgments on him, the traditional system of policed "undergraduate-type" courses, the fierce pressure of public competition—these are the things that break down a graduate student's confidence and feeling of worth. This is precisely what ought not to happen."[1] One might add to the reasons for loss of self-confidence the graduate student's peculiarly ambiguous economic situation.

From reading newspapers and magazines these days, a college senior is bound to conclude that attending a graduate school is considered almost a patriotic duty. The need for college teachers and researchers, he is told, is critical. Just as business and industry pay good starting salaries to attract college seniors, he thinks, so graduate schools will somehow manage to help him over his first years. He soon finds out that the path has not been wholly smoothed. The winners of generous and adequate fellowships are apt to think of themselves as the kind people in whom society is willing to invest money, and their self-confidence is thus strengthened. Others may be equally deserving, but the subject in which they are interested does not at the moment seem of great importance to society; or, more frequently, capricious circumstances which have nothing to do with the student's merits decree that this year student *A* will receive a fellowship, but student *B* will not. Consequently, student *B*, whose performance has been as good as student *A*'s, loses confidence either in himself or in the wisdom of those who award aid.

"Why should graduate students be protected from outrageous fortune," someone may ask, "when everybody else is subject to its slings and arrows?" Primarily because the graduate student's existence does not provide those shock absorbers which people in other situations find in the chance to leave for a more rewarding job. The graduate student, especially the future researcher, is usually so deeply committed to his field of special interest that he cannot seriously consider the alternative of choosing another. Often he has already invested so much time in graduate study that a move to another university, involving considerable loss of time and of academic credit, is not practical. Moreover, a graduate student may be—in fact he generally is—emotionally attached to his school to such an extent that going elsewhere does not seem to him desirable, even in a difficult financial situation.

The absolute and relative growth of graduate work mentioned

in the first chapter accounts for the fact that many graduate students are the first members of their family to follow an academic calling. Hence no family tradition exists of helping the student beyond college, nor does he like to accept money from home, even if it is offered or could be had. More than that: he may actually need a fellowship as encouraging his pioneering in new territory.

Besides, to an ever larger extent, graduate students are married. (A spotcheck made at Columbia during registration in the fall of 1956 found 36 percent of Columbia graduate students married, and 14 percent with children.) A census of graduate economics students at Columbia taken in the spring of 1956 listed 40 percent as married, and half of the married group with children.[2] It is idle to preach celibacy to young men and women whom we are asking to make many other sacrifices for their chosen vocation. Rather, our plans for the future must take the married student and his peculiar problems into account.

In many instances, before children arrive, a wife earns the mock degree of P.H.T., "putting husband through." In a society which generally expects the husband to provide for his wife it requires flexibility and courage to go against tradition. In some instances, when the wife is not wholly reconciled to the "abnormal" arrangement, the husband's ability to win at least a fellowship may become a far more important test of his worth than it deserves to be.

Those who are not close to graduate students have little conception of the physical and mental hardships under which many have to labor. The majority of graduate students in such fields as education and engineering are employed full time and do their graduate work at night and on Saturdays. Not many students in Columbia's Graduate Faculties are in this category, but in a few fields—usually those connected with teaching—they are. Even those who carry full programs are often diverted from their studies by outside work. Their plight is especially severe when the outside occupation has no relation to their studies, absorbs many hours each week, and requires long trips back and forth from job to home or to school. A symbol of the determined graduate student was an outstanding student in the Russian Institute who made his living as a longshoreman. The only time he complained about his lot was during a strike, when, in order to maintain his standing in the union, he had to report every day on the dock.

A full and clear picture of the financial support given to graduate students is difficult if not impossible to obtain. A recent federal publication on fellowships,[3] for example, lists only those fellowships offered by the institutions who answered the government's questionnaire—and everyone familiar with the flood of questionnaires engulfing deans, registrars, and departmental chairman knows that answers are not as reliable as they should be. Even if all answers were complete and accurate, a list of fellowships offered by institutions to their own students omits many other important sources. Fellowships offered by such organizations as Ford, Danforth, Southern Fellowships, Wenner-Gren, AAUW, and the American Council of Learned Societies are only a few of the fellowships offered by foundations; financial support is also offered by states such as New York; other fellowships come from industry and business, and last, but certainly not least, many substantial federal programs support graduate education, such as the annual National Science Foundation awards, Fulbright fellowships and the several thousand projected fellowships of the 1958 National Defense Education Act. The role played by government contract research, which in 1956–57 amounted to over 250 million dollars [4] is not widely known because many government research projects are "classified." To obtain a full picture of financial support through fellowships and other means within a given university such as Columbia would be a research job of considerable scope.

The situation is complicated not only by the scattering of fellowships. Financial aid is given to graduate students in many other forms, such as nominal graduate tuition charges at many state universities, teaching and research assistantships, and other jobs within the university ranging from floor swabbing to the making of bibliographies. Traditionally, and quite illogically, any money paid within the university is considered a form of aid, but money earned outside the university is not. Thus a student doubling as a part-time stock clerk in the university's paper store appears in statistics as receiving financial support, whereas another student who holds a teaching assistantship in a college a few blocks away does not. Even if a perfect system for reporting and classifying all financial aid were devised, it would still be most difficult to maintain a reliable count, for typically many positions including assistantships and even lectureships are assigned in the last minute and as the need arises.

No detailed study of financial support given to student in Columbia's Graduate Faculties during 1940 to 1956 is available, but in the fall of 1956 the President's Committee on the Educational Future of the University undertook a survey of fellowships and scholarships held by students in the academic year 1956–57.[5] It affords at least one example of the relative distribution of fellowship aid among the three Graduate Faculties. To anticipate its general conclusion, the social sciences and humanities fare less well than the sciences, a fact which has already been established many times before and which has recently been confirmed in the answers of Harvard Ph.D.'s to their Dean's questionnaire. Lack of money had a "considerable" lengthening effect on the time needed for the Ph.D. for 5 percent of students in the natural sciences, for 13 percent in the social sciences, and for 14 percent in the humanities.[6]

Twenty-three percent of all students registered in Columbia University and 32 percent of the students in the Graduate Faculties in the fall of 1956 received one of three forms of financial aid: a fellowship from Columbia, a fellowship from outside, or employment by Columbia. In the faculties of Political Science and Philosophy, paralleling the university average, 23.8 and 21.1 percent respectively of all students received aid in some form. The percentage of Pure Science students receiving aid, however, as in the national survey, was the highest in the university, namely 58.9, and surpassed even Columbia College's 51.2 percent. These percentages are roughly in line with the national picture. According to a survey undertaken in the spring of 1954,[7] by the National Science Foundation, 24 percent of all resident graduate students held stipends either in the form of teaching or research assistantships or fellowships from various sources such as foundations, the federal government, or the universities themselves. The median stipend was $1,285. But, as in the case of Columbia University, the differences between fields were marked. First of all, 41 percent of the students surveyed by the National Science Foundation were studying education; of this large group only 4 percent received any stipends, and their median stipend was $920. At the other extreme of the scale were 62 percent of the somewhat smaller group of students in life sciences who received stipends, the median being almost $1,400, and 58 percent of the students in the physical sciences, with a median stipend of $1,360.

The 1954 national survey, covering an estimated four-fifths of the entire graduate student population, found that students in the natural sciences and engineering, who accounted for about one-third of the graduate population, received over two-thirds of the fellowship money given to graduate students.[8] The distribution of fellowships in 1956–57 among the three Graduate Faculties of Columbia University is shown in Table 24. It should be noted that this distribution includes funds specifically earmarked by their original donors for given subject matters.

Table 24. AMOUNTS PAID TO THE GRADUATE FACULTIES FOR FELLOWSHIPS, 1956–57

Faculty	*Total amount from Columbia*	*Total amount from outside*
Philosophy	$ 46,890	$120,790
Political Science	69,000	228,250
Pure Science	113,230	167,062

Source: *Report of the President's Committee on the Educational Future of the University* (New York, 1957), p. 222.

With one exception, Pure Science held the largest relative share in all three forms of fellowships.

Table 25. GRADUATE STUDENTS RECEIVING FELLOWSHIPS OR EMPLOYMENT IN COLUMBIA UNIVERSITY 1956–57

Faculty	*Number of students registered 1956–57*	*Percent with Columbia fellowships*	*Percent with outside fellowships*	*Percent employed in Columbia*
Philosophy	1,095	4.3	8.1	9.0
Political Science	1,167	5.6	12.7	6.6
Pure Science	767	6.9	12.5	41.9

It must be added here that assistantships are more numerous in the sciences, from the nature of the subject matter, and this adds to the amount in the last column.

Pure Science stipends were higher on the average than those in the other faculties.

Table 26. AVERAGE AMOUNTS OF FELLOWSHIPS IN THE GRADUATE FACULTIES 1956–57

Faculty	*Average amount of Columbia fellowships*	*Average amount of outside fellowships*
Philosophy	$ 509	$ 719
Political Science	531	804
Pure Science	1,068	918

If any correlation between the size of fellowships and the quality of students should exist—and we have some reason to suspect that it does—then certain indications in Table 27 are disturbing. Some departments, it would appear, spread their already limited funds among many students rather than concentrating them on a few individuals, thereby perhaps failing to attract superior students in sufficient numbers. If such a practice were to continue over many years, an entire discipline might deteriorate for want of leaders.

Table 27. PERCENT OF GRADUATE STUDENTS WITH FELLOWSHIPS AND AMOUNT PER CAPITA, 1956–57

Department	*Students with fellowships (in percent)*	*Amount of fellowships per capita (in dollars)*
Zoology	35	$375
Geology	33	319
Chemistry	25	270
Sociology	23	221
Public Law	18	145
Economics	18	130
History	18	104
Mathematics	10	101
Anthropology	19	98
Physics	12	95
English	11	84
Philosophy	11	70
Psychology	9	47
Romance Languages	5	20

Source: *Report on the Educational Future of the University*, p. 223.

A 1954 national survey of financial support of graduate students established the fact that 77 percent of all stipends reported were for teaching and research assistantships.[9]

At Columbia in 1956, assistantships accounted for only 52 percent of all cases of financial support. In the humanities the difference was more marked: here 77 percent of all supported students in the national survey held teaching and research assistantships, as against 9 percent at Columbia; and 68 percent in the national survey in the social sciences, as against 6.6 percent at Columbia.

The relatively small share of assistantships at Columbia University can be explained by two facts: the Columbia Graduate Faculties number more students proportionately to the undergraduate college than is true at most universities, and it has long been a policy in Columbia College to use virtually no graduate students as teachers, except in science laboratory courses, or after they have completed all requirements for the Ph.D. except the dissertation.

Here the same 14 departments as in Table 27 are arranged according to the extent to which students in each were employed in 1956–57 within the University.

Table 28. GRADUATE STUDENTS EMPLOYED IN COLUMBIA 1956–57

Department	*Number of students registered*	*Percent employed in Columbia University*
Physics	196	59
Chemistry	110	51
Zoology	51	47
Geology	68	46
Psychology	96	21
Mathematics	88	18
Romance Languages	173	17
Sociology	98	17
Anthropology	101	10
Economics	186	9
English	506	8
Philosophy	132	6
Public Law	297	4
History	448	3

The 1956–57 Columbia survey established the fact that relatively few students received more than one form of aid at one time, but many changed from one form in one year to another in the next. At our present level of knowledge about financial support we can only speculate about the relative merits of the various forms of support. What is the relative advantage of employment over fellowship aid? Here a point made in Dean Elder's report is worth considering: a graduate student who by virtue of a job in the university becomes to some extent a partner in the educational enterprise is less apt to suffer from doubts about his worth than one who is a passive recipient of aid. On the other hand, as the need for instructors becomes more acute, many graduate schools connected with large undergraduate colleges are increasingly using graduate students as instructors, and also tend to place heavy teaching duties on them. Already certain institutions delay or even side-track graduate students in their quest for a degree, while in many cases subjecting undergraduates to inferior teaching; in the future more institutions, under the pressure of necessity, may engage in this practice. The need for fellowships—as against assistantships—may thus become more urgent as time goes on.

Financial support is certainly not the only, and possibly not even the decisive, factor contributing to the success of a graduate student. It would be misleading, for example, to claim that with greater financial support degrees in the humanities could ever be completed as rapidly as in some of the sciences. On the other hand, overgenerous support of graduate students in certain fields, notably the sciences, has been known to delay the completion of research because the candidates preferred fellowships to the offers of prospective employers. But it stands to reason that generally students who must support themselves have less time to spend on their graduate training, and that an increase in fellowship aid will at least shorten the time needed for degrees.

It is significant to note in this connection that, in 1956, 73 percent of Princeton University's graduate students received support through fellowships or assistantships, as against 32 percent at Columbia and 24 percent for the entire country in 1954. Princeton's graduate school allows only full-time students, and it is also known for its insistence on the rapid completion of the doctor's degree.[10] If there were any doubts about the connection between financial aid and time taken for the Ph.D., the following striking figures from our survey alone would make a case. The average time taken for the Ph.D. by nonveteran men in Columbia's Faculty of Political Science was 9.6 years, but it was only 7.4 years for veterans. In the Faculty of Philosophy an average 9.8 years was taken by nonveterans, but only 7.5 years by veterans; and in the faculty of Pure Science 6.1 years was taken by nonveterans, and 5.3 years by veterans. To some extent the time lapses indicated for veterans may be shortened by the statistical fact that more veterans in our study entered toward the end of the survey than did nonveterans. Those veterans who take many years for the doctor's degree are thus not averaged in, and veterans' time lapses appear shorter. But the effect of financial support on the length of time taken for the Ph.D. can be seen in another result of the study. Not only did the fully supported group of veterans complete the Ph.D. more rapidly, the gains were also most marked in the two faculties in which the nonveterans received the least support, and least marked in Pure Science where almost 60 percent of *all* students received fellowships or assistantships.

Any study of the performance of graduate students who have received fellowships is bound to show that they are more successful than a group without fellowships. But since fellowships are generally awarded to students of special abilities, the relative success of such students may prove little more than the skill of the awarding committees in selecting students of promise. It is fortunate that we can study a group of students who were subsidized without regard for their academic standing, the veterans.

Of the almost eight million veterans who took advantage of the education and training programs at a total cost to the country of over $14.5 billion, some 2.3 million attended colleges and universities.[11] In the winter of 1947–48, a total of 11,332 veterans were registered on the Morningside campus of Columbia University, over two thousand of these in the Graduate Faculties. (For a detailed count of veterans, see Tables 51 and 58.) Among the 14,928 men students surveyed who entered between 1940 and 1956, 6,638, or 44 percent, were veterans of the Second World War, and 616 were veterans of the Korean War.

In order to understand the conditions under which veterans attended graduate school, it is helpful to recall the main provisions of the so-called G.I. Bills concerned. The Servicemen's Readjustment Act of 1944, Public Law 346, which applied to the large majority of veterans of the Second World War at Columbia provided monthly subsistence pay of $75 for students without dependents, $105 for students with one dependent, and $120 for those with more than one dependent, provided the student was enrolled in a program full time, defined as registration for at least twelve points. In addition to this subsistence allowance, veterans were permitted to accept paid employment, provided their earnings did not exceed $135, $165, and $170 respectively in the three categories.

In addition to paying a subsistence allowance, Public Law 346 authorized payments for tuition, fees, books, and materials not to exceed $500 per academic year. Until the fall of 1948, since Columbia's tuition and fees amounted to under $500 a year, the allowance for tuition covered the entire cost. After that time the government's allowance fell short of paying the tuition bill. However, veterans were entitled to tuition benefits over $500 a year provided they were willing to apply future entitlements toward tuition. To pay $2.10 tuition, a student had to sacrifice one day of entitlement and the subsistence payments he would receive under the regular arrangement. Many veterans were unwilling to mortgage their future in this fashion, and each time tuition rates were raised some left the university while others reduced the number of credits they were carrying. Total entitlement for any veteran amounted to one year plus the number of months he had been in the service, not to exceed 48 calendar months.

In contrast to Public Law 346 of 1944 for Second World War veterans, Public Law 550 of 1952 for Korean War veterans made larger monthly payments to the student but did not provide separately for tuition. Whereas a veteran under Public Law 346 chose his college or university without regard to the tuition rate, Public Law 550 placed a veteran in a position comparable to that of any other student who in his choice of institution considers the cost of tuition. A full-time single student, defined by Public Law 550 as one registering for *14* or more points, could in 1952 attend Columbia full time provided he was willing to use up almost his entire training allowance for payment of tuition. Monthly training allowances for full-time students under Public Law 550 were $110 for single students, $135 for students with one dependent, and $160 for those with more than one dependent. Whereas rates for part-time students under Public Law 346 were simply prorated,

Public Law 550 provided part-time rates a little less than under a prorated schedule. Under Public Law 550 no ceiling was placed on the additional income a veteran could obtain from employment. Entitlement was calculated by allowing 1-1/2 days of training for each day in service, the total not to exceed 36 calendar months. Both laws allowed change of institutions as well as a certain amount of interruption of studies; both made it difficult to change to another field of studies.

Unless a veteran had stayed in the service after the end of hostilities, training under Public Law 346 had to be begun at the latest by July 25, 1951, and the law officially expired on July 25, 1956. Both laws recognized the fact that veterans in graduate status may be full-time students in the true meaning of the word, even though they are attending no classes. Supervised research in residence which occupies all of his time entitled a veteran to full benefits; if he devoted only part of his time to research, benefits were prorated in the same fashion as for students attending some classes. Public Law 346 required written certification of research by the adviser or the chairman of the department in question once every term, and Public Law 550 once a month. Thus many Ph.D. candidates were able to work on their dissertations while receiving full G.I. benefits.

As may be seen in detail in Table 51, male veterans of the Second World War made up anywhere from 3 to 53 percent of the classes entering between 1940 and 1955. For the purposes of our study the few women veterans have been counted with the other women students. Men who entered before the war, left, and returned as veterans, and those under the provisions of P.L. 16 for wounded veterans, were all tabulated as veterans, as were the negligible number of veterans who did not use their G.I. benefits. Often these veterans received New York state or other benefits instead, and in some instances they saved up their G.I. benefits for later use. Since fewer women students received Ph.D. degrees than men students, in the following tables veterans of the Second World War were compared only with nonveteran men; "nonveteran" refers always to male students who, so far as could be established, had not served in the armed services during the periods covered by Public Laws 346 or 550.

One measure of the relative merits of the veterans' as against the nonveterans' group is the percentage of both groups which by 1956 had earned no degrees. Since the number of Second World War veterans decreased sharply after 1951, figures for students newly registering after 1951 have been disregarded, for otherwise the picture would be distorted in favor of the veterans.

Table 29. MEN STUDENTS ENTERING 1940–51 AND EARNING NO DEGREES BY 1956

	Nonveteran men	*Second World War veterans*
Total entering 1940–51	6,070	5,763
Total without M.A. or Ph.D. degree by 1956	3,364	2,604
Percent	55	45

Since veterans' subsistence payments under Public Law 346 were geared to the numbers of points carried, veterans tended to register for fuller programs than nonveterans. A comparison of nonveteran men and Second World War veterans shows striking differences.

Table 30. MEN STUDENTS ENTERING 1940–55 AND COMPLETING 40 OR MORE POINTS BY 1956 (*In percent*)

Year of entrance	*Nonveteran men*	*Second World War veterans*
1940	14	56
1941	12	63
1942	20	41
1943	20	67
1944	20	39
1945	26	43
1946	33	51
1947	33	49
1948	28	43
1949	24	44
1950	21	37
1951	22	25
1952	19	13
1953	13	14
1954	4	0
1955	0	0

Since many Ph.D.'s earn Master's degrees on the way, Master's degrees earned by those who had also earned Ph.D.'s have been disregarded in most our our tabulations.

Veterans entering before 1950 had a better record in earning master's degrees than did nonveterans, but from 1951 on the performance of nonveterans was superior.

As a group, the post-1951 veterans were probably less good than those who had begun graduate studies earlier. Only those veterans of the Second World War who entered the Graduate Faculties after 1951 and who had been enlisted for further service after the cessation of hostilities retained their eligibility for the benefits of Public Law 346. The group which arrived after 1951 was thus made up of men who after the war had chosen a paid position in the armed

Table 31. MEN STUDENTS ENTERING 1940–55 AND EARNING M.A. BY 1956 (EXCLUDES THOSE WHO ALSO EARNED PH.D.)

Year of entrance	*Nonveteran men*		*Second World War veterans*	
	Number	*Percent*	*Number*	*Percent*
1940	149	30	20	51
1941	79	20	15	47
1942	68	26	10	34
1943	56	20	8	44
1944	73	22	16	52
1945	102	29	50	37
1946	187	38	411	48
1947	179	43	361	50
1948	110	37	377	48
1949	218	38	346	46
1950	209	34	191	33
1951	165	36	126	23
1952	159	37	44	18
1953	93	30	26	18
1954	36	19	6	11
1955	3	9	0	0

services, rather than enter college or graduate school. Eventually they left their military jobs, either because they chose to or because they were dismissed.

Undoubtedly many promising students developed an interest in graduate work after first trying an army career, and undoubtedly servicemen were discharged irrespective of their merits simply because there were no more jobs for them. But the veterans group entering earlier probably had a higher proportion of outstanding and eager individuals than did the group arriving later.

Public Law 346 encouraged registration in courses by tying subsistence payments to the course load. Nonveterans who believed that they were not doing well in their studies tended to lighten their course loads or to leave the university after the M.A., whereas veterans tended to stay on. Table 32 supports this assumption.

Table 32. MEN STUDENTS ENTERING 1940–55, EARNING M.A. BY 1956 AND TAKING 40 OR MORE POINTS (*In percent*)

Year of entrance	*Nonveteran men*	*Second World War veterans*
1940	31	70 *
1941	28	80 *
1942	56	70 *
1943	52	0 *
1944	55	38 *
1945	53	60
1946	49	68
1947	47	61
1948	40	54
1949	36	54
1950	32	46
1951	28	40
1952	30	23 *
1953	23	23 *
1954	3 *	0 *
1955	0 *	0 *

* Percentage based on a group smaller than 50.

Table 32 applies to students who had earned a master's degree, though not a Ph.D., and who thus had received some encouragement to go on. The difference between veterans and nonveterans becomes even more pronounced when we look at those who by 1956 had received neither an M.A. nor a Ph.D. degree. Table 33 demonstrates dramatically the need for careful counseling of graduate students whenever they are subsidized for attending classes. The "satisfactory progress" often demanded by those who provide support should be interpreted most conscientiously by those judging students' progress.

The classes entering after 1951 have had relatively less time and fewer chances to earn master's or doctor's degrees. They also included a high proportion of nonveterans, so that tabulations of students entering from 1940 to 1956 would be bound to show the veterans in a more favorable light. Table 34, therefore, includes only figures for the classes entering between 1940 and 1951. Since

Table 33. MEN STUDENTS ENTERING 1940–55, EARNING NO DEGREES BY 1956 AND TAKING 40 OR MORE POINTS (*In percent*)

Year of entrance	*Nonveteran men*	*Second World War veterans*
1940	8	42 *
1941	8	47 *
1942	8	26 *
1943	12	40 *
1944	10	40 *
1945	15	32
1946	23	35
1947	23	36
1948	21	32
1949	17	35
1950	16	33
1951	19	21
1952	13	10
1953	9	12
1954	4	0 *
1955	0 *	0 *

* Percentage based on a group smaller than 50.

Table 34. MEN STUDENTS ENTERING 1940–51 AND EARNING PH.D. BY 1956 (*In percent*)

Department	*Nonveteran men*	*Second World War veterans*
	PURE SCIENCE	
Chemistry	34	42
Geology	31	39
Mathematics	5	5
Physics	18	23
Psychology	18	33
Zoology	24	31
	POLITICAL SCIENCE	
Anthropology	18	23
Economics	6	12
History	12	13
Mathematical Statistics	9	7
Public Law	6	10
Sociology	9	8
	PHILOSOPHY	
English	5	7
Fine Arts	3 *	9 *
French	19	21
Philosophy	15	19
Religion	31	24
Spanish	7	7

* Percentage based on a group smaller than 50.

most veterans entered after 1945, a smaller percentage might be expected to earn degrees by 1956. The figures in Table 34 thus present a dramatic plea for the financial support of graduate study.

In Table 35, departments of instruction are arranged in order by the percentage of veterans in the total male population of each department. In the absence of questionnaire studies we can only

Table 35. VETERANS ENTERING 1940–51, AS PERCENT OF TOTAL MALE POPULATION OF EACH DEPARTMENT

Department	*Number*	*Percent*
English	1,266	61
Geography	35	59
History	732	56
Fine Arts	45	55
Sociology	321	52
Public Law	596	52
Italian	23	52
Mathematical Statistics	118	52
Anthropology	98	49
French	129	49
Spanish	103	49
Music	51	49
Geology	129	48
Economics	571	47
Philosophy	213	44
Medical Science	93	44
Physics	251	43
Chemistry	207	40
Mathematics	184	39
Psychology	129	38
Engineering	143	37
Zoology	55	36
German	35	30
Religion	66	25
Christian Education	15	18

speculate on the reasons why veterans preferred certain departments over others.

Of the students who received no Ph.D. degrees a certain proportion, varying greatly from department to department, received master's degrees. The differences between veterans and nonveterans were sometimes pronounced, but generally the two groups showed only slight differences; generally, a slightly higher percentage of veterans received master's degrees.

In a few departments, however, the differences were notable. The figures in Table 36 for the departments of Music and Fine

Table 36. DEPARTMENTS IN WHICH NONVETERANS WERE LESS SUCCESSFUL THAN VETERANS (*In percent*)

Department	*Nonveteran men with M.A. by 1956*	*Second World War veterans with M.A. by 1956*
Physics	24	37
Economics	33	43
English	38	48
Music	36	61
Fine Arts	21	35

Arts are especially significant because both departments consider the M.A. an important degree, one which is not easy to earn. They require of their master's degree candidates a minimum residence of two years. The disparity in English is also significant, because in that field the master's degree is relatively more useful as a means to a teaching post than it is in other fields. In a few departments veterans were relatively less successful in earning master's degrees than were nonveterans; these were Zoology, Anthropology, Mathematical Statistics, and the basic Medical Sciences.

In comparing veterans with nonveterans we might conceivably compare primarily different age groups, for clearly veterans as a group are older than nonveterans. Let us therefore compare the

Table 37. COMPARISON OF SUCCESS OF NONVETERANS AND VETERANS, BY AGE-AT-ENTRANCE GROUP AND FACULTY. CLASSES ENTERING 1946, 1947, AND 1948

Age-at-entrance group	*Nonveterans*		*Veterans*	
	Total	*Percent earning Ph.D. by 1956*	*Total*	*Percent earning Ph.D. by 1956*
		PURE SCIENCE		
20 and under	49	37 *	16	44 *
21–23	110	29	177	33
24–29	200	32	395	33
30 and over	93	14	61	26
		POLITICAL SCIENCE		
20 and under	36	17 *	12	25 *
21–23	126	10	226	11
24–29	230	14	835	14
30 and over	160	9	226	18
		PHILOSOPHY		
20 and under	35	11 *	10	10 *
21–23	117	6	153	7
24–29	163	18	622	13
30 and over	96	22	191	13

* Percentage based on a group smaller than 50.

performance of veterans in given age groups with that of nonveterans in the same age groups, taking the three classes entering in 1946, 1947, and 1948 as a sample. More details may be obtained from an analysis of Table 54.

Like most figures about complex human situations, the case for financial support of graduate students is not fully clinched by our tabulations. Veterans differed from the nonveterans in respects other than that of being supported. To begin with, more were married; until we have studies comparing married with unmarried students, we cannot say to what extent the moral support of a wife and the feeling of responsibility for her future contribute to success in graduate school. Furthermore, as many who have taught veterans will testify, veterans as a group seemed to know better than the nonveterans what they wanted, and to go about getting it in a more determined manner. Veterans probably had more of an opportunity to think through their plans for graduate work; they did not pass from college into graduate school, as do so many nonveterans. And finally, professors undoubtedly tended to be more lenient toward veterans, especially soon after the war.

Chapter Five. FUNCTIONS OF A GRADUATE SCHOOL

IN THE CURRENT preoccupation with the Ph.D. it is easy to lose sight of the functions of a graduate school other than training Ph.D.'s. A graduate school is primarily a family of scholars who select their own company, setting their own climate of interests, and supporting each other in their quest for more knowledge. To enable them to do research the scholars need libraries and laboratories. For financial support and intellectual stimulus they surround themselves with apprentices. Those apprentices who give a good account of themselves are rewarded with a title—doctor of philosophy—but this rewarding of apprentices is only a secondary interest of any graduate school.

Today, since society foresees a need for more teachers and researchers at the Ph.D. level, the business of training Ph.D.'s receives more attention than that of advancing research. But reforming the Ph.D., though it will not bring the millennium, is an important chore which will benefit the entire complex called graduate education. First of all, like all reforms, it will produce the kind of information contained in this book. Second, a reform will bring about more conscious planning than in the past, and as a result, better use of the precious time of graduate teachers. Finally, reform may improve the entire atmosphere of graduate education. Neglect of the young people who have come to him as disciples has given many a graduate teacher a bad conscience. Facing a task which he knows he has neglected will set his mind free for the important business of scholarship.

Recently the discussion of gradute work has been focussed on the report of four deans of graduate schools who had been asked to prepare it for the Association of Graduate Schools. The report published in the New York *Times* of November 13, 1957, suggested that ideally the Ph.D. degree ought to be completed after three years of graduate study. While it may not be possible to reduce the time span quite so ruthlessly, a conscious effort to shorten the time will certainly contribute toward reducing the shortage of Ph.D.'s.

THE DOCTOR OF PHILOSOPHY

Table 38 arranges thirteen large departments according to the extent to which students who entered between 1940 and 1956 had earned Ph.D. degrees by 1956. If we arrange the same departments

Table 38. AVERAGE TIME SPENT BY STUDENTS ENTERING 13 DEPARTMENTS 1940–56 AND EARNING PH.D. BY 1956

Department	*Ph.D.'s (in percent)*	*Average time (in years)*
Chemistry	28.0	5.3
Geology	25.0	6.6
Religion	19.0	5.4
Psychology	15.0	5.5
Physics	14.0	7.0
Philosophy	10.0	7.4
French	10.0	9.7
History	7.0	9.5
Economics	6.0	8.8
Public Law	5.0	8.1
Sociology	5.0	10.1
English	3.3	10.1
Mathematics	3.0	7.4

in the order of the average time students take for the Ph.D., eleven departments occupy the same place in the list or are one or two numbers away from their place on the first list. Only French and mathematics are far out of place.

If the time taken for the Ph.D. can be curtailed, graduate schools may be able to produce 10 or 20 or even 50 percent more Ph.D.'s every year without increasing library and laboratory facilities, and without markedly enlarging the teaching staff. Moreover, since Ph.D. candidates who are delayed in their quest for the degree are apt to leave graduate school for other occupations, it is reasonable to suppose that a tightening up of Ph.D. requirements will result in a larger number trained.

In Tables 56 and 57, which show the length of time taken for

Ph.D.'s earned between 1940 and 1956, the year given is that when the Ph.D. degree was earned, and not, as in the rest of the book, the year when the student entered the Graduate Faculties. Again, other tables in the study refer to about 90 percent of the students enrolled, but tables in the Ph.D. figures are based on between 98 and 99 percent of the actual Ph.D.'s awarded.

The time a student took to earn his degree was calculated by subtracting the year in which he entered from the year in which the degree was awarded. Thus a student listed as taking five years might have entered in February, 1950, and earned his degree in December, 1955, taking in fact almost six years; or he could have entered in September, 1950, and earned his degree in January, 1955, taking only a little over four years. Since most students enter in September and most Ph.D.'s are awarded in June, and since the bulk of the time lapses was computed from many individual cases, the variations concealed by our way of computing may be disregarded.

We noted that students who began their studies with light programs tended to leave the university without earning a degree. Yet there did not seem to be any relation between the length of time taken for the Ph.D. and the fact that students started on a full program. Students who needed many years lost much of their time between their last official registration and the award of the degree—in other words, research and the writing of the dissertation accounted for most of the long delays. Typically, students who took inordinately long accepted a job far from the university, after completing the residence requirements.

The question remains, why is the average time needed for the Ph.D. in Chemistry half as long as in English? Why is the average in Slavic almost half of the average time of the Ph.D. in Germanic Languages? To answer such questions we need first to know a great deal more than we do now about the role of departmental requirements and departmental customs. For example, does a dissertation topic freely chosen by a student require considerably more time than one assigned by the sponsor? To what extent are students delayed by intradepartmental disagreements on the propriety of a topic or the adequacy of its treatment? Does the day-by-day check on a Science student's research in a laboratory save him the time which the Social Science and Humanities major loses when he has submitted his first draft, and an overburdened sponsor postpones, perhaps for months, the reading of it? Or is the most important factor the assiduity with which the student presses forward? If this should be true, does the financial reward at the end of the journey toward the Ph.D. account for at least some of a candidate's drive? It may be no accident that the fields which offer high salaries for Ph.D.'s are generally the same in which candidates finish up rapidly. At the same time, it is notorious that a first rate student who has passed his orals brilliantly can, in any field, obtain a position before writing his thesis, and is thus prevented, year after year, from completing his work for the degree.

We have already established the fact that a larger number of those who entered graduate work young obtained Ph.D.'s than of those entering at a more advanced age. Yet those who entered after the age of 23 took less time to finish than did the younger candidates, and those who entered after 29 finished in even less time. In the absence of studies of individuals, we can only guess at the explanation.

It is possible that older students, being more aware how time flies, make a more determined effort to conclude. The less determined may well be prevented by the weaknesses of middle and old age from ever finishing. This would explain the relatively high proportion of failures among the older group.

Those who enter when they are older may be better prepared than the younger students in the sense that they have had time to read and assimilate the large bodies of knowledge necessary for passing examinations and doing research in the discipline. The strikingly short average lapse of time for those entering language departments at the age of 30 or more would bear this out. The same reasoning may apply to the History Department, in which the mastery of large masses of factual detail is more imperative than in other political sciences. Experience may thus be more important. But in a field such as mathematics, which requires less factual knowledge than the other sciences, and where students entering relatively late have slight chances of success, those older students

Table 39. YEARS SPENT BY STUDENTS EARNING PH.D., EXPRESSED AS PERCENT OF TOTAL PH.D. DEGREES

Category	Total Ph.D.'s	Mean time (in years)	2 years or less	3 years	4 years	5 years	6 years	7 years	8 years	9 years	10 years	11–14 years	15–18 years	19 years or more
10 percent sample before 1940	182	8.2	4	8	12	9	12	7	7	8	4	15	8	6
Pure Science, 1941–56	1,219	6.0	5	14	19	18	14	9	5	4	3	5	2	0
Political Science, 1941–56	899	8.9	2	4	10	11	12	10	10	7	7	14	7	6
Philosophy, 1941–56	718	9.4	3	4	8	9	10	10	9	9	7	17	8	6
Subcommittees, 1941–56	105	5.3	16	10	21	15	10	5	11	5	1	3	1	1

Table 40. AVERAGE YEARS SPENT BY STUDENTS EARNING PH.D., BY VARIOUS CATEGORIES

Category	Total Ph.D.'s	Total group	Nonveteran men	Veterans	Women	Born in New York	All born in United States	Foreign born
10 percent sample before 1940	182	8.2	7.6	0	9.6	9.3 *	8.0	8.2 *
Pure Science, 1941–56	1,219	6.0	6.1	5.4	6.4	6.1	6.1	5.2
Political Science, 1941–56	899	8.9	9.6	7.4	10.2	9.6	8.8	8.0
Philosophy, 1941–56	718	9.4	9.8	7.5	11.0	10.2	9.2	8.8
Subcommittees, 1941–56	105	5.3	5.3	5.6 *	4.3 *	5.6 *	5.5	4.8 *

* Average based on a group smaller than 50.

who obtained a doctor's degree did so in considerably less time than candidates who had entered young. In physics, too, those entering late finished more rapidly than the younger group.

Candidates entering graduate school when they are older are presumably already employed as teachers in a college. They have probably been urged by their elders to earn a doctor's degree so as

Table 41. AVERAGE YEARS SPENT BY STUDENTS EARNING PH.D., BY AGE-AT-ENTRANCE GROUPS (*Total of cases averaged*)

	Under 20		*20–23*		*24–29*		*30 and over*	
Department	*Number*	*Average*	*Number*	*Average*	*Number*	*Average*	*Number*	*Average*
PURE SCIENCE								
Biochemistry	2	8.0	29	6.6	24	4.9	6	4.3
Botany	..	...	20	6.7	28	6.9	5	4.6
Chemistry	16	5.9	187	5.5	126	4.9	14	5.1
Geology	3	6.7	59	7.3	65	6.0	12	6.2
Mathematics	5	10.0	25	7.7	12	6.2	2	5.0
Physics	7	6.1	80	7.1	53	6.9	2	6.0
Psychology	6	7.2	80	5.8	54	4.8	15	4.9
Zoology	4	9.0	36	6.9	24	5.2	8	7.4
POLITICAL SCIENCE								
Anthropology	2	11.2	28	9.8	37	6.5	18	5.7
Economics	4	13.3	80	9.3	90	8.4	31	7.8
History	10	10.7	123	10.1	137	9.4	56	7.9
Public Law	1	12.0	58	10.1	55	6.9	33	6.5
Sociology	3	10.7	32	11.3	39	9.0	26	9.0
PHILOSOPHY								
Chinese and Japanese	..	...	1	10.0	11	8.3	9	6.4
English	3	12.0	92	11.8	109	9.6	46	7.9
Fine Arts	..	...	7	13.0	3	12.0	5	7.0
French	2	11.5	53	11.2	47	9.1	34	7.8
German	1	38.0	12	14.6	13	11.9	6	7.7
Music	1	4.0	2	8.5	5	8.4	1	10.0
Philosophy	3	8.0	41	8.7	62	6.8	24	6.5
Religion	1	5.0	6	7.2	42	5.8	37	4.6

to qualify for promotion to a position with tenure. As a group, these men and women are at least partly urged on by others rather than by themselves; they are under considerably stronger pressures to finish up than those who set their own deadlines.

Finally an older group may be safely assumed to have more money than a young group. This is certainly true of veterans, whose relatively shorter spans of degree earning are partly responsible for the low averages of our older groups, especially those beginning between 24 and 29.

We do not as yet know enough to be able to advise individual students to defer entrance into graduate school until they have acquired a broader knowledge of their field and a greater experience of life, or have found out enough about the financial rewards of a Ph.D. to want one badly, or saved enough money to be able to go through graduate school on a full time schedule, without interruptions or part-time work. But in advising young people who have the option of, say, presenting themselves for induction or entering graduate school, the figures in Tables 41 and 57 may argue in favor of delaying entrance into graduate work.

Table 42 compares the time intervals between first registration and award of the Ph.D. at Harvard and at Columbia. Since the

Table 42. COMPARISON OF TIME INTERVALS BETWEEN FIRST REGISTRATION AND AWARDING OF PH.D., HARVARD AND COLUMBIA (*In percent*)

	Pure Science		*Political Science*		*Humanities*	
	Harvard 1950–54	*Columbia 1940–56*	*Harvard 1950–54*	*Columbia 1940–56*	*Harvard 1950–54*	*Columbia 1940–56*
2 years or less	4	5	1	2	1	3
3 years	18	14	7	4	8	4
4 years	40	19	27	10	14	8
5 years	22	18	20	11	19	9
6 years	5	14	17	12	19	10
7 years	4	9	8	10	6	10
8–10 years	3	12	6	24	12	25
Over 10 years	4	7	14	27	21	31
	100	98	100	100	100	100

Source: J. P. Elder, *A Criticism of the Graduate School of Arts and Sciences in Harvard University and Radcliffe College* (Cambridge, 1958), Appendix II, p. 34.

figures for Columbia are based on Ph.D.'s earned between 1940 and 1956, whereas Harvard's are for the years 1950 to 1954, Harvard's time lapses could be expected to be shorter, for in the years 1950 to 1954 relatively large percentages of Ph.D.'s were earned by veterans whose circumstances enabled them to take less time. Furthermore, while the figures for Columbia are for about 99 percent of the entire group of Ph.D.'s earned, Harvard's figures are based on a questionnaire which was returned by only 88 percent of those addressed, quite possibly a relatively more successful group than the 12 percent who failed to answer. On this count, too, the Harvard figures could be expected to show a shorter span.

We can also compare Harvard's average times for 1954 Ph.D. candidates in the social sciences with Columbia's figures (shown in parentheses) for Ph.D.'s earned between 1940 and 1956. Anthropology 11.2 years at Harvard (7.5), Economics 7.3 years (8.8), Government 8.1 (8.1), History 8.1 (9.5), Psychology 7.0 (5.5), Social Relations 7.5 (Sociology 10.1).[1] Harvard's graduate school does not include women in its statistics because Harvard's women students are organized as an administratively separate group called Radcliffe; women at Columbia tended to take longer for their Ph.D.'s than men, and quite possibly Radcliffe students do likewise. Finally, since Harvard controls and restricts part-time study more methodically than Columbia, Harvard's students may be expected to devote a relatively larger share of their time to their studies and thus to finish more rapidly. In spite of these factors, students in Columbia departments of Anthropology and Psychology actually took less time toward their degrees than Harvard students and at several points along the scale showed marked superiority in speed. The causes remain obscure.

A 1958 survey completed by the Dean of Harvard's Graduate School of Arts and Sciences isolated the following problems connected with delays in graduate education: (1) the language requirement (it delayed 16 percent of the men in the natural sciences, 20 percent of those in the social sciences and 27 percent of those in the humanities). (2) Research and the writing of the thesis delayed "considerably" 43 percent in the natural sciences, 44 percent in the social sciences, and 38 percent in the humanities. (3) Lack of money had a "considerable" delaying effect for 5 percent in the natural sciences, 13 percent in the social sciences, and 14 percent in the humanities. (4) "Considerable" delays were caused by teaching fellowships for 12 percent in the natural sciences, 8 percent in the social sciences, and 16 percent in the humanities. Other delaying factors mentioned were: academic ennui, love of Cambridge, and psychiatric trouble. (These were not, of course, interrelated.)

Future research will have to compare findings at different universities before an attempt can be made to isolate reasons for delay. An interesting experiment by the Economics Department at Yale, for example, should answer the question whether it is practicable to reduce the time for an economics doctorate to four years. Princeton's impressively low averages may be connected with the large amount of financial aid available at Princeton, and are perhaps partly due to Princeton's small departmental contingents. Yet "attrition," i.e. failure to obtain a degree, even at Princeton accounts for between 30 and 40 percent. Clearly, many other questions must be asked that will be found hard to answer.

To what extent, for example, do averages of time elapsed reflect on the department's policy toward borderline students? If a department tells its weak candidates reasonably early that they should not proceed further, it will have fewer Ph.D.'s taking a long time than a department which allows candidates of doubtful merit to keep trying.

A given department, which may come down in a given instance to a single man who is chairman, may be more concerned with getting candidates through than with the quality of their training. In that event the short time lapses for Ph.D. candidates may reflect only the low quality of the work done. On the other hand, the early identification of promising Ph.D. candidates—this is singularly true in Columbia's department of Anthropology—will affect favorably the average time elapsed.

Differences in subject matter and study conditions undoubtedly have significant effects: the extent, for example, to which a student works in a laboratory, in a setting similar to a German *Seminar* in library carrels or reading rooms, or at home; the frequency of contacts between student and teacher and, closely related to this question, the average number of Ph.D. candidates each instructor sponsors; the severity of the language examinations; the amount of factual information required in certifying examinations; the extent to which entering students have been given sound training in their chosen fields while still undergraduates; the prevailing opinion in the department about what constitutes respectable size for a doctoral dissertation; the degree to which as undergraduates the candidates have been trained in the ways of independent research; the amount of literature which has to be surveyed before staking out a dissertation topic; the extent to which primary and secondary sources are accessible, or proper laboratory equipment obtained; the need to explore parts of the topic which turn out to be unworkable, unimportant, or unoriginal; the climate of interest in the topic being explored, and connected with that, the number of fellow students who are willing to discuss the dissertation with its author; finally such mundane factors as the distance between a student's room and his place of study and experimentation, the nearness of convenient eating and lounging facilities, the opportunities for physical exercise--all these factors have a bearing on the ease and speed with which a doctoral degree can be achieved.

An obvious answer to the problem of the time-wasting Ph.D. is a time limit. If a candidate knows that three or four or five years after entering graduate school he must finish his degree he will naturally make a more serious effort than under a system which allows him, as does Columbia, to present himself for a degree whenever he is ready. A time limit, far from creating an unnatural, academic condition actually simulates the natural atmosphere of a deadline under which all those operate who write for publishers, for learned journals, or for professional meetings. The question is whether the prevailing method of offering "all the world and time" to a candidate is not an unfair temptation to all parties concerned, the student who writes and the sponsor who is supposed to read. Certainly the great universities, such as Yale, which set a seven-year maximum do not seem to harm the cause for which all graduate schools are striving with equal sincerity. However, just as an understanding publisher will extend deadlines for a dilatory but valuable author, so an understanding department or dean must be ready to waive the rule for the exceptional candidate. Administered by a rigid or unsympathetic person a time limit may become a dangerous weapon. Talent can be hamstrung, quality compromised, and departments rushed into bad judgments by the ticking of the timepiece.

THE MASTER OF ARTS

The master's program, as we saw in Chapter One, grew more rapidly in numbers than the doctoral. Between 1900 and 1950, there was a thirty-seven-fold increase in master's degrees but only an eighteen-fold increase in doctor's degrees. Only about one out of every seven graduate degrees was a doctor's degree.[2]

While the master's degree grew throughout the country, Columbia's share dropped from a high of 17.7 percent in 1915 to 0.8 percent in 1956, as can be seen in detail in Table 43.

Not only did the master's degree awarded by Columbia's Graduate Faculties account for a smaller share of the national total, it also made up an increasingly smaller share of Columbia's total graduate degrees. This development was in line with the Faculty's inclinations and interests. In 1957, the Committee on the Educational Future of the University recommended that the Graduate Faculties concentrate to an even larger extent on the doctor's degree. The Committee was partly led to its recommendation by the argument that many metropolitan schools offered master's programs.

The supporters of the master's degree offer a number of arguments. First of all, as the report of a committee of fifteen assembled under the auspices of the Fund for the Advancement of Education indicated,[3] there is bound to be such a demand for college teachers very soon that whether the graduate schools like it or not, many of their M.A. graduates will be drawn into teaching and kept so busy that they will not have time to earn their doctor's degrees.

A second argument applies especially in such disciplines as English, where for successful teaching a wide range of knowledge is more important than the ability to do original research. Champions of the master's as a terminal degree point out that a college teacher who can enlarge the scope of his reading will be better prepared for teaching than one who must in his first years of teaching devote all his spare time to research and writing for the doctorate.

Thirdly, the proponents of the M.A. point out that an even greater part of the college population during the 1960s will be freshmen and sophomores, many of them in junior colleges. Accordingly, relatively more college teachers with master's degrees will be needed than with the doctorate. For, rightly or wrongly, college administrators who want highly trained teachers for upper-

Table 43. COLUMBIA'S PERCENTAGE OF NATIONAL TOTAL EARNED M.A. DEGREES IN LIBERAL ARTS SUBJECTS, 1904–55

Year	*Columbia total*	*Columbia percentage*
1904	160	9.5
1905	197	10.2
1906	178	10.0
1907	190	11.7
1908	219	11.1
1909	212	9.7
1910	289	13.7
1911	315	12.8
1912	370	12.2
1913	504	16.7
1914	492	15.1
1915	633	17.7
1916	410	10.5
1917	389	11.4
1918	281	9.7
1919	241	6.7
1920	403	9.4
1921	381	7.4
1922	448	7.5
1923	519	7.3
1924	495	6.0
1925	513	5.6
1926	503	4.9
1927	558	5.1
1928	629	5.2
1929	623	4.7
1930	684	4.7
1931	632	3.7
1932	700	3.6
1933	628	3.3
1934	588	3.2
1935	521	2.9
1936	540	3.0
1937	494	2.5
1938	476	2.2
1939	516	2.1
1940	521	2.0
1941	430	1.7
1942	360	1.5
1943	244	1.3
1944	259	1.9
1945	258	1.6
1946	364	1.9
1947	839	2.7
1948	892	2.1
1949	920	1.8
1950	935	1.6
1951	824	1.3
1952	662	1.0
1953	594	1.0
1954	504	0.9
1955	472	0.8
1956	479	0.8

classmen accept less well trained teachers for freshmen and sophomores.

It is not possible to say accurately how many students enter graduate work at Columbia University with the intention of going no further than the master's degree. A modest student may set himself the limited objective of a master's degree, without realizing that eventually he would like to earn the Ph.D. Another student may announce that he wants a doctorate in the mistaken notion that his chances of admission will be improved by this announcement. Without asking students about their intentions we can make good guesses by finding out to what extent they have registered for courses beyond the requirements for the master's degree.

Of the 4,725 students who between the years 1940 and 1956 entered the English department, a total of 1,856 earned master's and doctor's degrees, and 2,869 no degrees at all. Of the 1,705

Table 44. TOTAL NUMBER OF PH.D. DEGREES EARNED BY 1956 BY STUDENTS ENTERING 1940–56 AND PERCENT ALSO EARNING M.A.

Department	*Total Ph.D.'s earned by 1956*	*Percent also earning M.A.*
	PURE SCIENCE	
Chemistry	251	68
Geology	105	41
Mathematics	26	50 [a]
Physics	121	36
Psychology	112	29
Zoology	53	66
	POLITICAL SCIENCE	
Anthropology	62	10 [b]
Economics	119	50
History	185	61
Public Law	103	50
Sociology	61	74
	PHILOSOPHY	
English	151	64
Fine Arts	8	38 [a]
French	84	46
Music	7	43 [a]
Philosophy	89	47
Religion	81	11 [b]
Spanish	25	44 [a]

[a] Percentage based on a group smaller than 50.

[b] Anthropology and Religion have clearly separated programs for master's and Ph.D. candidates and generally admit students to one or the other.

who earned master's degrees, 247, or 15 percent, took more courses than were needed for a master's degree. Of the large group which took no degrees, only 122, or 4 percent, took enough courses to indicate that they very likely aspired to the doctor's degree. In other words, in the entire group of a little under five thousand, only 8 percent can clearly be said to have given evidence of wanting to proceed toward the Ph.D. and of having failed along the way. A small number of master's degrees in our survey were taken by Ph.D. candidates and were not counted in the M.A. statistics. Table 44 shows to what extent those who earned Ph.D.'s had also earned master's degrees.

As a detailed analysis of the Ph.D.'s earned in 1956 shows, only one-fifth held no master's degrees of any kind. Table 45 omits, as do all other tables, Ph.D.'s in Education which originate in Teachers College.

Table 45. NUMBER OF STUDENTS AWARDED PH.D. IN 1956 WHO HELD MASTER'S DEGREE

Ph.D. degrees awarded in Columbia University in 1956			243
Master's degrees from Columbia			118
	M.A.	105	
	M.S.	11	
	M.B.A.	2	
Master's degrees from other institutions			71
	M.A.	53	
	M.S.	13	
	M.B.A.	3	
	M.F.A.	2	
No master's degree			54

The minimum time prescribed for a master's degree in the Graduate Faculties is two semesters. A student entering in the fall of 1940 could earn his master's degree at the earliest at the 1941 Commencement, and was counted as having taken one year. If he needed a third full semester he received his degree in February, 1942, and was counted as having taken two years.

About three-fourths of all those who earned master's degrees did so within two years—only during the war years, when many students had to interrupt their studies for military service, did more than one-fourth of all those earning degrees take more than

Table 46. YEARS SPENT BY STUDENTS EARNING M.A. (*In percent*)

Year of entrance	*1–2 years*	*3 years*	*4 years*	*5 years*	*6 years or more*
1940	75	7	3	4	11
1941	66	8	6	7	13
1942	60	14	9	6	10
1943	57	21	10	6	5
1944	63	16	9	5	7
1945	73	12	6	4	5
1946	76	11	5	3	4
1947	76	13	4	2	4
1948	78	11	4	4	2
1949	75	11	5	4	3
1950	75	11	7	4	*
1951	77	12	7		
1952	81	13	*	*	
1953	81	*			

* Complete figures were not available.

two years. As more time elapsed, fewer and fewer students completed their master's degrees—around 15 percent after 3 years, around 6 percent after 4 years, around 5 percent after 5 years. Of the 366 M.A.'s earned by those who entered in 1940, only 35 were awarded between 1946 and 1956, and only 27 of the total 273 awarded to the class entering in 1941 were given after six or more years.

Table 47. NONVETERAN MEN WITHOUT PH.D. BY 1956 AND NOT REGISTERED IN 1955–56

Year of entrance	*Total entering*	*Percent with enough points for M.A.*	*Percent with M.A.*	*Percent of M.A.'s completing 40 points or more*	*Percent without degree completing*	
					40 points or more	*30–39 points*
1940	505	46	30	31	8	19
1941	389	36	20	28	8	14
1942	260	40	26	56	8	12
1943	277	40	20	52	12	14
1944	325	41	22	55	10	15
1945	353	50	29	53	15	16
1946	495	64	38	49	23	21
1947	419	66	43	47	23	21
1948	298	66	37	40	21	27
1949	573	67	38	36	17	34
1950	608	61	34	32	16	30
1951	457	60	36	28	19	27
1952	432	63	37	30	13	32
1953	310	54	30	23	9	29
1954	192	43	19	3	4	29

Tables 47, 48, and 49 show to what extent nonveteran men, veterans, and women who by July, 1956, had not received Ph.D. degrees had registered for at least enough points to earn a master's degree, and how many were successful in earning one.

Relatively fewer M.A.'s were earned by those who entered in the war years; the reason may be that many were drafted or entered jobs, and then did not return to graduate school. But this explanation should not apply to women, whose absolute numbers increased toward the end of the war, and whose relative share in

Table 48. SECOND WORLD WAR VETERANS WITHOUT PH.D. BY 1956 AND NOT REGISTERED IN 1955–56

Year of entrance	*Total entering*	*Percent with enough points for M.A.*	*Percent with M.A.*	*Percent of M.A.'s completing 40 points or more*	*Percent without degree completing 40 points or more*	*Percent without degree completing 30–39 points*
1940	39	85	51	70	42	26
1941	32	88	47	80	47	29
1942	29	66	34	70	26	26
1943	18	72	44	0	40	10
1944	31	74	52	38	40	13
1945	134	70	37	60	32	20
1946	865	74	48	68	35	18
1947	725	79	50	61	36	24
1948	789	80	48	54	32	30
1949	758	80	46	54	35	32
1950	574	76	33	46	33	33
1951	541	61	23	40	21	29
1952	239	44	18	23	10	24
1953	148	43	18	23	12	23
1954	53	32	11	0	0	28

the total graduate population also rose steeply in the war years (see Table 51). Here we may assume that admissions standards were lowered during the war. And it is safe to conclude from the steep rise in the success ratios for nonveterans after the war that they too had been screened less severely during the war than after.

The tables further show to what extent students registered well beyond the 30-point total required for a master's degree without earning a Ph.D. degree. Both nonveteran men and veterans took points beyond those required for the master's degree to a much larger extent than women students, of whom a larger percentage obviously were satisfied to leave the university with a master's degree.

From 1950 on, fewer students completed 40 and more points simply because they had fewer years in which to accumulate points than did the group which had started earlier.

As discussed in detail in Chapter four, the veterans of the Second World War were paid subsistence on the basis of points taken and thus were rewarded for taking full programs. This fact explains why relatively more veterans took enough points for a

Table 49. WOMEN WITHOUT PH.D. BY 1956 AND NOT REGISTERED IN 1955–56

Year of entrance	*Total entering*	*Percent with enough points for M.A.*	*Percent with M.A.*	*Percent of M.A.'s completing 40 points or more*	*Percent without degree completing*	
					40 points or more	*30–39 points*
1940	454	48	33	27	5	20
1941	434	45	28	26	4	21
1942	339	43	29	31	6	15
1943	460	43	28	32	6	17
1944	668	45	28	28	6	19
1945	764	49	33	21	8	20
1946	694	62	38	32	12	29
1947	534	64	42	30	13	29
1948	421	60	37	23	10	30
1949	439	56	40	18	10	30
1950	394	62	40	24	12	32
1951	356	56	31	20	11	27
1952	370	54	29	26	10	28
1953	329	44	23	8	5	30
1954	193	28	11	5	1	22

master's degree without earning one, and why relatively more veterans who had not obtained a master's degree continued well beyond the minimum required for the master's without earning a doctor's degree.

When we compare nonveteran men with women who took enough points for a master's degree without receiving one, we find in most years a slightly larger percentage of women. Two possible explanations could be hazarded for this phenomenon: (1) women have little trouble completing courses but tend, a little more than men, to stumble over the essay requirement; (2) relatively more women enter those departments requiring a master's essay than do men. The latter predominate in the science departments, which do not require a master's essay. Thus a slightly larger percentage of the women may be expected fail after having actually completed the necessary points, because a larger share of women had to complete essays.

Chapter Six. SUMMING UP

THE CURRENT INTEREST in graduate schools rests on the projected need of colleges and universities for more teaching and administrative talent. After what has been said about the dearth of facts, it is not surprising to find that those who guess at future needs recognize their handicap. Two issues of the same annual, *Current Issues in Higher Education,* published by the Association for Higher Education, differ as much as 60 percent in their estimates for teachers. The 1954 issue (p. 49) and the 1956 issue (p. 211) give these estimates of the needed number of full-time college and university faculty members:

	1954 estimate	*1956 estimate*
Needed in 1960	158,000	268,000
Needed in 1965	208,000	350,000
Needed in 1970	245,000	414,000

The 1954 estimate assumes that in 1952 there were 130,000 full-time faculty members; the later study, including part-time teachers in its estimate, speaks of 200,000 full-time *equivalent* teachers in 1952–53.

Another report, *The Graduate School Today and Tomorrow,* published in December, 1955, projects even larger demands. In order to maintain the present student-teacher ratio of one to thirteen, it says, we shall need 250,000 college teachers by 1960, 345,000 by 1965, and 495,000 by 1970: "To expect," says the report (p. 7), "that by 1970 the proportion of college teachers holding the Ph.D. degree will have declined from the present 40 percent to 20 percent is not statistical hysteria but grassroot arithmetic."

To what extent do colleges today expect their faculties to hold

Ph.D. degrees? A 1954 study of the National Education Association found the following requirements for degrees: [1]

Grade	*Percent of institutions requiring Ph.D.*	*Percent of teachers who hold Ph.D.*
Instructor	3.1	11
Assistant Professor	14.7	29.7
Associate Professor	43.7	46.4
Full Professor	84	71.4

All statements to the contrary notwithstanding, many institutions in employing new men are more anxious to improve their Ph.D. quota than to bring good teachers into their class-rooms. Accordingly, the extent to which colleges hire Ph.D.'s is some measure of the supply of Ph.D.'s for teaching positions. As the pickings grow slim, the proportion of Ph.D.'s among newly hired faculty members will drop.

In 1953–54, 40.5 percent of the full-time teaching staff in American colleges and universities held doctor's degrees taken in course,[2] and only 10.4 percent held less than a master's degree. Of the *newly hired* faculty members in the same year, 31.4 percent held Ph.D.'s. In the next three years the percentages of Ph.D.'s among new faculty members decreased to 28.4 percent, 26.7 percent, and 23.5 percent in 1956–57—a clear indication of a rapid drop in the supply of Ph.D.'s. In 1953–54, 18.2 percent of new faculty members had less education than a master degree. In the next three years the percentage rose to 19.3, 20.1, and 23.1 percent respectively. To fill vacancies, colleges and universities had to hire an increasing percentage of men and women who had not even earned a master's degree.

While it is possible to form an idea of the coming need for college teachers in all fields combined, to predict with any assurance how many Ph.D.'s will be needed in particular fields is impossible. What colleges need and what circumstances will force them to accept are two different things, and moreover fields are scarcely comparable. The accompanying excerpts from a table published in 1957 show how in a span of four years the proportion of Ph.D. holders among newly hired faculty decreased, and how some fields were affected more, or sooner, than others.

Field	1953–54	1954–55	1955–56	1956–57
	Percent having Ph.D. in			
Biological Sciences	54.5	60.1	56.5	51.2
Physical Sciences	53.0	46.9	46.3	43.7
Mathematics	34.2	29.3	27.3	20.5
Psychology	68.4	62.5	59.2	55.3
Social Sciences	42.4	44.9	41.5	33.7
English	29.0	23.4	18.9	17.7
Foreign Langauges	36.3	32.5	35.6	27.9
Philosophy	46.7	41.6	51.9	38.4

(*Teacher Supply and Demand in Colleges and Universities 1955–56 and 1956–57* [National Education Association, 1957], p. 19.)

It is easy to predict that the deterioration in such fields as English, Psychology, the Physical Sciences and Mathematics will continue; for these fields, and especially English, are immediately affected when large freshmen classes enter. The demands for scientists and mathematicians may be suddenly accelerated by the sudden demands of industry. Within one year, for example, after the start of the Korean War, the government increased its demand for physicists tenfold, and the number of industrial openings for physicists in February 1952 was ten times as high as it had been two years earlier.[3] The demand of government agencies for social scientists also grew spectacularly in the forties and early fifties,[4] and it may grow again. In other fields, such as foreign languages, the deterioration has begun only recently and will in all likelihood continue.

Shortages may make themselves felt quite suddenly in certain fields because it is impossible to use teachers in these fields at all unless they have been thoroughly trained. In other fields, relatively untrained teachers can do at least a creditable job teaching elementary classes. In the absence of a census of future demands for college teachers in given fields, an accurate accounting of the percentage of Ph.D.'s among newly hired faculty members by fields may serve at least as an index of the demand in those areas. A finer analysis by departments (instead of the broader categories used by the NEA) would be of greater service. As it is, the critical need for economists, for example, is statistically neutralized by the larger figures for other fields, such as History and Political Science, which under the heading of "Social Sciences" are counted in with Economics.

The general situation may, to be sure, improve not by the training of more Ph.D's but by the enhanced quality of the M.A.'s. But the benefits of whatever reforms to be undertaken in M.A. programs may be offset by the secondary schools' demand for M.A.'s trained in subject matter rather than in the methods of education. If this should happen—and there are good reasons for thinking it likely—the graduate schools will not only have to train master's candidates more carefully, they will also have more masters to train.

At the same time even though more teaching positions will be filled with teachers without a doctor's degree, the demand for Ph.D.'s will be increased by two other factors. Professor Rabi of Columbia has said that high-school teachers of Physics, in order to present their material with adequate understanding, must have a training at least of the scope and intensity of a Ph.D. In more and more fields, particularly in the sciences, the amount of subject matter to be mastered has grown to such an extent that to know less than what can be learned in a doctor's program is deemed useless.

The demand for Ph.D.'s will be further increased by a development which Lloyd S. Woodburne has described.[5] As the field of higher education becomes more complex, fewer heads of departments will be personally acquainted with their colleagues in graduate schools who have trained applicants for teaching positions. Lacking the confidence which existed in times of closer personal contacts, the standard label of the Ph.D. will therefore appear more necessary to those who hire new faculty.

In our highly integrated society communication is swift. Desired changes, being passed from mouth to mouth and from report to report quickly assume unjustified and unjustifiable authority and proportions. America is impatient by temperament, and prefers immediate relief to slow deliberation. And the press is apt to sharpen whatever needs attention. Finally, the concentration of large sums of money in a few strategic places, such as the Department of Defense or certain corporations or foundations, enables a few men to make their will felt instantly. It would not be in the interest of our country if by such means rapid changes in the distribution of graduate students among the many fields of specialization were brought about.

Perhaps it is helpful to remember that even a planned society cannot plan exactly for the complex structure called Higher Education. In a debate with three American university presidents, Dr. Peter Polukhin of the Soviet Ministry of Education admitted that he was quite satisfied if his estimates of the future needs for specialists were out no more than 25 percent.[6]

In this one connection alone, our ignorance of detail may well be bliss, for it keeps us from planning too minutely. We can be sure that the demand for manpower trained in graduate schools is increasing and will continue to grow, but we cannot predict with any assurance in what fields the demand will be heavy, in what light, what new fields will appear, what others will dwindle. The emphasis therefore must be on strengthening graduate training as a whole, rather than in special fields.

A Policy for Scientific and Professional Manpower concludes that planning must never become narrow. It states that the demand for scientific and professional personnel will continue to be high, but warns that arithmetical estimates of the size of the demand for each group within that larger group ten or twenty years hence are not possible. "In the absence of much more precise knowledge or of willingness by a society to forego the fulfillment of certain goals in favor of others, attempts to rank manpower groups according to some hierarchy of importance are hardly feasible." [7]

Have we any reason to expect help other than that which we can provide by reforms within the graduate schools? And if any relief is in sight, what is it to be? The U.S. Commissioner of Education, Lawrence G. Derthick, in a major policy speech before the National Conference on Higher Education in the spring of 1958 considered "the expansion and strengthening of graduate education and the provision of Federal fellowships for potential college teachers" one of the three critical points in a program of federal aid to education—the two others being the conservation of talent and foreign language instruction.[8] This interest on the part of the executive branch is reflected in the National Defense Education Act, which includes fellowships and loans for graduate students and which was signed by the President on September 2, 1958. Equally heartening are the bold program undertaken by the State of New York for supporting graduate students who want to become college teachers and the extension of the National Science Foundation's scope. A step was taken on a national scale by the Ford Foundation when, in 1957, by a grant of 24.5 million dollars it enabled the Woodrow Wilson Fellowship program to expand its offerings and award a thousand fellowships annually for five years to prospective college teachers entering graduate schools.

Other forms of help may materialize more slowly, but they are worth thinking about. One is the supply of talented college teachers from the faculties of secondary schools. Even now, though to a small extent, high school and preparatory school teachers transfer to college faculties. As more secondary school teachers obtain master's degrees a larger percentage may after some years of service in secondary schools seek employment in colleges. This transfer will undoubtedly be facilitated by the steady and sometimes spectacular growth of junior colleges, which will act as natural stepping stones from high school to college employment. Increased mobility among teachers across the arbitary boundary line between secondary and higher education may be a good thing not only for higher education, but may also make secondary education attractive to all those who upon graduation from college would accept a teaching post in secondary schools were it not for the fear of being frozen in a career they mistakenly consider dull.

Graduate education may well begin to recruit students from colleges which have not in the past sent on many graduates. In this process the new federal scholarships are bound to be an incentive.

Women account for about one-third of the master's degrees awarded every year, and for about 10 percent of the doctor's degrees.[9] In 1955, women made up one-third of the total teaching staff of teacher's colleges but only 14 percent of the regular full-time staff in private universities.[10] The president of the Scientific Manpower Commission, John S. Nicholas of Yale, predicted (New York *Times*, 11-2-57) that within five years 25 percent of the country's college teachers would be women, rather than 8 percent as now.

What are the prospects for drafting more women into college teaching? 80 percent of over seven hundred institutions answering a questionnaire of the National Education Association said that they were willing to employ more women as college teachers.[11]

The figures in Table 59 suggest that as a group women are a poor risk as doctoral candidates, but do nearly as well as, and in some fields better than, nonveteran men in earning master's degrees. If college teachers of the future are going to be recruited from M.A.'s, then women may well plan an increasingly important role. And the figures in Table 59 may well reflect a local rather than a national situation, for the young women who come to Columbia often seek a year or two in the stimulating atmosphere of New York City rather than a degree.

A more serious argument against women as a potential source of college teachers is offered by those who say that it is economically unsound to spend money on training workers whose professional usefulness will be cut short by marriage. Of over two thousand women who in June, 1951, received master's degrees throughout the nation, almost 10 percent were housewives by June, 1952.[12] However, as keeping house has become less of a chore than it was fifty years ago, and as it may continue to take less and less time, more housewives are able to continue their jobs outside the home, with the exception perhaps of the years when the children are young.

Another possibility might be the development of a new teaching degree beyond the master's level but less specialized than the doctor's degree and not requiring a long dissertation. This degree would make it unnecessary for the prospective college teacher to complete the long and hazardous trip to the Ph.D. but at the same time afford him a knowledge of his subject similar to that of a doctoral candidate who has passed the difficult departmental examinations before research. Such a teaching degree would take a minimum of two and a maximum of four years. However, it is highly improbable that any degree other than the doctorate would ever be accepted by the academic community as "different but equal," even though accrediting agencies might be persuaded to omit the counting of Ph.D's from their rating procedure.

The most important relief, things being what they are, will come when college teachers' salaries are such that they seriously appeal to young people who today are attracted into medicine, law, and business. Here it is important to note that significant improvements have been made and continue to be made. By 1957, according to Professor Seymour P. Harris of Harvard, an authority on the subject of faculty salaries, "a large part of the loss of purchasing power [of the teaching profession] had been recouped." [13] A 1958 study made by the National Education Association showed these striking percents of increase over two years for median salaries in all colleges and universities: [14]

Rank	*Percent of increase 1955–56 to 1957–58*
Professors	14.1
Associate Professors	14.5
Assistant Professors	13.7
Instructors	11.6

The same publication, incidentally shows that gains were largest in municipal universities (22.9 percent) and smallest (10.6 percent) in privately endowed universities.

But, as Professor Harris warns us, we are still far from the point where we can relax our efforts. "Even if salaries are increased by 50 percent in the next few years and 95 percent in ten years, the faculty members will have lost about $2 billion since 1940 as a result of the failure of salaries to keep up with the cost of living . . . and perhaps $5–6 billion . . . as a result of the failure of salaries to keep up with the pay rise of the average member of the labor market. If the serious lags of the past continue, and past losses are not recouped, the quality of college faculties is bound to suffer." [15]

At this moment in their history, graduate schools need tables of figures, so they may understand better what has happened in the past. They need rules for the derelict, time limits for the laggards, and money for those who are hampered by the need to make a living. But tables can be drawn, rules can be written, time limits set, and even money, in God's own good time, will be raised. What is more needed is not widely wanted, because it can be neither measured nor seen. Thoreau, when he went to Walden Pond, found such a thing—a new perspective on an old, familiar scene.

The ideas suggested by the facts and figures given in the preceding chapters may help create order where confusion reigned before. But they will only bring about cleanliness, not godliness. A graduate school, like a military outfit, should be judged not by anything that can be seen, measured, or organized, but by its spirit.

This spirit does not exist abstractly but is lodged in the living men and women who are part of the graduate enterprise. To be important, a book about graduate students would have to deal not with averages and groups, but with the men and women whose lives are dedicated to graduate work—whose lives *are* the graduate school.

A disillusioned view of these people was taken many years ago by a Chicago professor. William E. Dodd's opinion is not shared by many, but it deserves quoting for its sobering effect. "The ambitious young folk enter business," he says, "for that leads to what modern society calls success, the handling of vast sums of money or evidences of money. The second class or even the third class of young folk enter upon the professions, perhaps the lesser lights upon the profession of teaching. Business dulls and deadens the mind of the capable; the professions lead into high specializations (medicine, law) or into a slow broadening of the mind of the less intellectual (preaching, teaching, and writing). What we have then is to take in the main the poorest material and make of it the thinking element of the country." [16]

At the other extreme stand those who emphasize the dedication and the idealism of advanced study. Albert Einstein, in writing about another scientist, Max Planck, spoke of the "emotional condition" which made achievements such as Planck's possible and compared it to that of the religious devotee or the lover.[17] And President DuBridge of the California Institute of Technology used almost identical words: "Being attracted to physics is very much like falling in love. It is almost unexplainable and an almost emotional experience." [18]

Any reforms based on Professor Dodd's dispondent assumptions will fail because they misunderstand the nature of one who searches after truth. Any true reform of graduate study must be based on respect and affection for the graduate student. All planning is faulty if it is concerned with large figures but neglects the tremendous changes which may be brought about by one gifted individual. ". . . men like Einstein, Toscanini, or General Marshall are always in short supply. They must be excluded from any consideration of shortages of normal men. To exclude them, however, does not solve the difficulty, for the presence of a great creative genius in the supply of any group of professionals or scientists can completely alter the character of the demand by changing the nature of the problem with which the group is concerned." [19]

Possibly those who refuse to listen when the graduate student's plight is explained realize that the graduate student by definition stands at the edge of present and future, at the edge of the status quo and of a new way of life. Perhaps they are dimly aware of the paradoxes of his existence.

As a prospective teacher, the graduate student must live close to his contemporaries, must not get too far ahead of his pupils, must transmit those values upon which our society is based. As a researcher, however, he must live in isolation from his fellow men, must proceed without concern for his audience, must risk the perils of a trip into uncharted territory, beyond the good and evil of his own heritage. As one training or ready to be a teacher he must have an eye on the calendar—if not on the clock—for colleges are waiting to hire him and they need him badly. But as a true researcher he must live outside time, without regard for the passing of weeks and months and years, concerned only to know the truth.

As the graduate student stands in a paradoxical relation to his society, so the graduate school also must play a dual role. It is not only an agency to further the objectives of society; it is also the instrument through which society renews and overcomes itself. The graduate school simultaneously serves and rules, conforms and rebels. The paradox of its existence demands that it seek out what society wants, but at the same time that it proceed without regard for immediate needs. It serves best when it is independent, and is fruitfully independent only when its serves.

The graduate school's location inside and outside society accounts for the irregular and fortuitous manner in which it is supported by society. It also explains why so often the graduate student is harrassed rather than serene, involved in detail rather than steeped in wisdom, driven to his tasks like a slave rather than choosing his work like a free man. A man on the edge needs and seeks limited and prescribed tasks, loves the things which bind him to reality, and welcomes prescribed tasks because they excuse him from the lonely excursions into new territory. Many graduate students today are described by Thoreau's strictures of his contemporaries: "restless committed men, whose time was all taken up in getting a living or keeping it." A new way of being and working is wanted today, not only for the graduate student, but for all those who, like him, stand at the edge.

NOTES

NOTES TO ONE: INTRODUCTION

1. *Second Report to the President, July, 1957* (Washington, D. C., 1957), p. 15.
2. National Science Foundation, *Graduate Student Enrollment and Support in American Universities and Colleges, 1954* (Washington, D. C., 1957), p. 2.
3. United States Department of Health, Education and Welfare, *Earned Degrees Conferred by Higher Educational Institutions, 1956–1957,* Circular No. 527 (Washington, D. C., 1958).
4. Fund for the Advancement of Education, *Teachers for Tomorrow,* Bulletin 2 (New York, 1955), p. 25.
5. *Ibid.,* p. 55.
6. *Ibid.,* p. 24.
7. Edited by F. W. Ness (Washington, D. C., 1957).

NOTES TO TWO: COLLEGES OF BACCALAUREATE ORIGIN AND AREAS OF BIRTH

1. Translated by Moses Hadas (New York, 1956), p. 359.
2. Marcia Edwards, *Studies in American Graduate Education* (New York, 1944).
3. *Ibid.,* p. 2.
4. *Graduate Student Enrollment and Support,* p. 11.
5. *Ibid.,* p. 16.
6. *The Geography of Certain Phases of Graduate Instruction in the United States* (Chicago, 1945), p. 117.

NOTES TO FOUR: FINANCIAL SUPPORT FOR GRADUATE STUDENTS

1. J. P. Elder, *A Criticism of the Graduate School of Arts and Sciences in Harvard University and Radcliffe College* (Cambridge, Mass., 1958), p. 21.
2. "Census of Graduate Economics Students," Bulletin No. 2 (typescript), August 1, 1956.
3. United States Department of Health, Education and Welfare, *Financial Aid for College Students: Graduate,* Bulletin 17 (Washington, D. C., 1957).
4. *Second Report to the President,* p. 99.
5. Donald Cafiero, "Report on Fellowships and Scholarships" (dittographed), March 15, 1957.
6. Elder, *A Criticism,* p. 72.
7. *Graduate Student Enrollment and Support.*
8. *Ibid.,* p. 19.

9. *Ibid.,* p. 22.

10. Letter to the author from the Department of Public Information, Princeton University, December 9, 1956.

11. *Second Report to the President,* p. 96.

NOTES TO FIVE: FUNCTIONS OF A GRADUATE SCHOOL

1. "The Behavioral Sciences at Harvard, A Report by a Faculty Committee" (June, 1954), p. 328.

2. William A. Jaracz, "Trends in Graduate Education," *Higher Education,* XI (February, 1955), 87–89.

3. *The Graduate School Today and Tomorrow, Reflections for the Profession's Consideration* (New York, 1955).

NOTES TO SIX: SUMMING UP

1. "Instructional Staff Practices and Policies in Degree-Granting Institutions, 1953–1954," *NEA Research Bulletin* XXXII (December, 1954), 166–76.

2. National Education Association, *Teacher Supply and Demand in Colleges and Universities 1955–56 and 1956–57* (Washington, D. C., 1957), p. 17.

3. National Manpower Council, *A Policy for Scientific and Professional Manpower* (New York, 1953), p. 195.

4. United States Department of Labor, *Employment Outlook in the Social Sciences,* Bulletin 1167 (Washington, D. C., 1954), p. 38.

5. *Faculty Personnel Policies in Higher Education* (New York, 1950), *passim.*

6. Kermit Lansner, ed., *Second Rate Brains* (New York, 1958), p. 50.

7. *Policy for Scientific and Professional Manpower,* pp. 245–46.

8. Address before the Thirteenth National Conference on Higher Education, Chicago, March 5, 1958. Reprinted in *School and Society,* May 10, 1958.

9. *Teacher Supply and Demand,* pp. 27 f.

10. National Manpower Council, *Womanpower* (New York, 1957), p. 283.

11. *Teacher Supply and Demand,* pp. 44 f.

12. National Science Foundation, *Education and Employment Specialization in 1952 of June 1951 College Graduates* (Washington, D. C., 1955), p. 48.

13. "Faculty Salaries," *AAUP Bulletin,* December, 1957, p. 582. See also the same author's "College Salaries, Financing of Higher Education and Management of Institutions of Higher Learning," *AAUP Bulletin,* September, 1958.

14. National Education Association, *Salaries Paid and Salary Practices in Universities, Colleges and Junior Colleges, 1957–58* (Washington, D. C., 1958), p. 9.

15. "Faculty Salaries," p. 590.

16. Quoted in Logan Wilson, *The Academic Man* (New York, 1942), pp. 17–18.

17. J. W. N. Sullivan, *The Limitations of Science* (New York, 1934), p. 265.

18. *Policy for Scientific and Professional Manpower,* p. 185.

19. *Ibid.,* p. 153.

APPENDIX

Table 50. TOTAL REGISTRATION IN COLUMBIA GRADUATE FACULTIES 1920–55

Year	*Winter Session*	*Spring Session*	*Net Total Attending*
1919–20	1,074	984	1,249
1920–21	1,099	1,072	1,303
1921–22	1,326	1,243	1,520
1922–23	1,635	1,543	1,872
1923–24	1,725	1,672	1,905
1924–25	1,905	1,640	2,264
1925–26	1,902	1,787	2,270
1926–27	2,228	2,199	2,724
1927–28	2,450	2,236	2,932
1928–29	2,509	2,312	2,973
1929–30	2,695	2,603	3,247
1930–31	2,709	2,592	3,275
1931–32	2,869	2,615	3,385
1932–33	2,763	2,457	3,205
1933–34	2,524	2,262	2,907
1934–35	2,427	2,242	2,862
1935–36	2,362	2,207	2,765
1936–37	2,346	2,241	2,735
1937–38	2,428	2,225	2,787
1938–39	2,741	2,491	3,178
1939–40	2,482	2,279	2,888
1940–41	2,327	2,056	2,660
1941–42	1,929	1,625	2,212
1942–43	1,397	1,225	1,665
1943–44	1,460	1,395	1,829
1944–45	1,767	1,741	2,193
1945–46	2,371	2,894	3,481
1946–47	3,918	3,973	4,584
1947–48	4,267	4,154	4,849
1948–49	4,126	4,116	4,770
1949–50	4,513	4,422	5,152
1950–51	4,323	4,234	4,994
1951–52	4,209	3,938	4,714
1952–53	3,617	3,391	4,108
1953–54	3,271	3,102	3,704
1954–55	3,098	2,970	3,577

Table 51. TOTAL RECORDS SURVEYED, STUDENTS ENTERING 1940–55

Year of entrance	Number surveyed	Percentages: Registrar's total	Spring starters	Summer starters	Fall starters	Non-veteran men	Second World War veterans	Korean War veterans	Veterans of both wars	Non-veteran Women	Women veterans	Number earning M.A. by 1956	Percent of total	Number earning Ph.D. by 1956	Percent of total
1940	1,133	97	19	14	67	52	6	0	0	42	0	366	32	122	11
1941	985	96	19	13	68	47	6	0	0	47	0	273	28	119	12
1942	725	91	22	20	58	42	8	0	0	50	1	219	30	91	12
1943	848	92	19	15	66	39	3	0	0	58	0	232	27	79	9
1944	1,151	96	21	17	63	34	3	0	0	62	0	336	29	107	9
1945	1,411	96	20	11	69	30	13	0	0	56	1	476	34	133	9
1946	2,560	93	29	13	59	26	45	0	0	28	1	1,126	44	422	16
1947	2,026	93	23	15	62	26	45	0	0	27	1	920	45	265	13
1948	1,812	89	21	14	66	21	53	0	0	24	1	779	43	214	12
1949	2,124	94	19	10	71	32	44	1	0	22	1	898	42	184	9
1950	1,925	97	21	9	70	37	38	2	1	22	1	698	36	119	6
1951	1,717	95	24	16	60	35	38	2	1	22	2	547	32	98	6
1952	1,359	94	22	12	65	42	22	2	1	31	1	441	32	38	3
1953	1,290	96	18	7	75	40	18	7	2	33	1	394	31	20	2
1954	1,175	94	20	10	70	43	12	11	2	31	1	280	24	10	1
1955	1,257	96	19	10	72	41	11	16	3	29	0	130	10	3	2
Totals	23,498		5,048 or 21%	2,916 or 12%	15,534 or 66%	8,175 or 35%	6,575 or 28%	537 or 2%	148 or ½%	7,417 or 32%	208 or 1%				

Table 52. INSTITUTIONS SENDING AT LEAST FIVE ALUMNI TO COLUMBIA GRADUATE FACULTIES 1940–56

Note: Parenthetical figures following state names indicate total number of institutions in that state sending students to Columbia Graduate Faculties.

	Total	*Ph.D.'s earned*	*M.A.'s earned*
AMERICAN UNIVERSITIES			
ALABAMA (16)			
Alabama Polytechnic Inst.	7	1	4
Alabama, Univ. of	40	1	18
Birmingham-Southern College	7	0	1
Talladega College	9	0	1
ARIZONA (3)			
Arizona, Univ. of	28	3	8
ARKANSAS (9)			
Arkansas, Univ. of	14	0	3
Hendrix College	10	1	3
CALIFORNIA (31)			
California Inst. of Technology	24	9	4
California, Univ. of (all campuses)	293	38	73
Mills College	11	0	1
Occidental College	20	1	9
College of the Pacific	5	0	4
Pomona College	33	6	9
Redlands, Univ. of	5	1	0
San Diego State College	5	0	0
Scripps College	9	0	4
Southern California, Univ. of	52	8	11
Stanford Univ.	93	4	37
COLORADO (6)			
Colorado College	10	0	4
Colorado School of Mines	10	3	3
Colorado State College of Education	5	0	3
Colorado, Univ. of	46	1	15
Denver, Univ. of	28	3	7
CONNECTICUT (15)			
Albertus Magnus College	6	0	1
Bridgeport, Univ. of	8	0	2
Connecticut College	36	0	13
Teachers College of Connecticut	8	0	3
Connecticut, Univ. of	43	5	12
St. Joseph College	5	0	2
Trinity College	31	2	11
Wesleyan University	64	13	22
Yale University	267	22	81
DELAWARE (2)			
Delaware, Univ. of	16	2	4
DISTRICT OF COLUMBIA (17)			
American University	12	1	5
Catholic University of America	27	1	10
Georgetown University	46	2	13
George Washington University	82	12	33

Table 52. INSTITUTIONS SENDING AT LEAST FIVE ALUMNI TO COLUMBIA GRADUATE FACULTIES 1940–56 (*Continued*)

	Total	*Ph.D.'s earned*	*M.A.'s earned*
AMERICAN UNIVERSITIES			
Howard University	43	2	13
Trinity College	18	0	9
FLORIDA (10)			
Florida Southern College	5	0	2
Florida State University	10	1	3
Florida, Univ. of	23	2	2
Miami, Univ. of	50	4	10
Rollins College	11	0	1
GEORGIA (23)			
Agnes Scott College	10	0	3
Emory University	35	2	7
Georgia Inst. of Technology	18	2	3
Georgia, Univ. of	27	1	10
Morehouse College	6	0	0
Oglethorpe Univ.	5	0	1
Piedmont College	5	1	1
Spelman College	5	0	1
IDAHO (3)			
ILLINOIS (49)			
Augustana College	8	0	1
Chicago, University of	180	17	51
Elmhurst College	11	4	1
Illinois College	5	0	2
Illinois Inst. of Technology	9	3	0
Illinois, Univ. of	112	11	24
Knox College	5	1	1
Lake Forest College	5	0	1
Loyola University	6	0	2
Monmouth College	5	1	2
North Central College	9	2	1
Northwestern University	95	5	30
The Principia	7	0	2
Roosevelt University	16	0	8
Wheaton College	30	5	13
INDIANA (21)			
Butler University	9	0	3
Depauw University	21	3	8
Earlham College	6	0	2
Indiana University	50	6	16
Notre Dame, Univ. of	48	0	17
Purdue University	33	4	5
Saint Mary's College (Notre Dame)	6	0	1
Wabash College	15	3	5
IOWA (23)			
Central College	6	2	1
Coe College	16	2	5
Cornell College	14	1	9
Drake University	10	0	4

Table 52. INSTITUTIONS SENDING AT LEAST FIVE ALUMNI TO COLUMBIA GRADUATE FACULTIES 1940–56 (*Continued*)

	Total	*Ph.D.'s earned*	*M.A.'s earned*
AMERICAN UNIVERSITIES			
Dubuque, Univ. of	7	0	2
Grinnell College	29	3	13
Iowa State College of A & M Arts	8	4	2
Iowa State Teachers College	5	2	2
Iowa, State Univ. of	82	14	22
Morningside College	6	1	3
KANSAS (16)			
Baker University	6	1	0
Kansas State College of Agriculture & Applied Science	8	0	5
Kansas, Univ. of	38	3	7
Southwestern College	5	0	2
Washburn Univ. of Topeka	5	0	2
Wichita, Municipal Univ. of	10	0	4
KENTUCKY (14)			
Asbury College	8	1	2
Berea College	13	2	2
Kentucky, Univ. of	36	5	10
Louisville, Univ. of	29	1	10
Transylvania College	5	0	1
LOUISIANA (16)			
Centenary College	5	0	0
Louisiana State Univ. and A & M College	29	3	7
Tulane University of Louisiana	35	0	10
MAINE (5)			
Bates College	28	4	7
Bowdoin College	66	5	29
Colby College	32	1	15
Maine, Univ. of	31	3	5
MARYLAND (18)			
Goucher College	30	1	14
Hood College	9	0	1
Johns Hopkins University	54	9	8
Maryland, Univ. of	29	0	6
Morgan State College	12	0	1
Saint John's College	12	2	5
U. S. Naval Academy	14	0	6
Western Maryland College	8	0	4
Woodstock College and Seminary	11	6	0
MASSACHUSETTS (49)			
American International College	6	0	3
Amherst College	103	14	30
Atlantic Union College	6	0	4
Boston College	21	1	8
Boston University	68	2	30
Brandeis University	12	1	3
Clark University	26	1	10
Emerson College	5	0	2

Table 52. INSTITUTIONS SENDING AT LEAST FIVE ALUMNI TO COLUMBIA GRADUATE FACULTIES 1940–56 (*Continued*)

	Total	*Ph.D.'s earned*	*M.A.'s earned*
AMERICAN UNIVERSITIES			
Harvard University	425	48	127
College of the Holy Cross	36	4	10
Massachusetts Inst. of Technology	98	19	32
Massachusetts, Univ. of	32	2	17
Mount Holyoke College	135	4	45
Radcliffe College	112	5	38
Simmons College	19	1	6
Smith College	204	15	51
Springfield College	7	0	2
Tufts College	53	5	14
Wellesley College	168	5	65
Wheaton College	28	1	16
Williams College	81	9	27
Worcester Polytechnic Institute	8	4	0
MICHIGAN (23)			
Alma College	5	0	1
Calvin College	11	0	3
Detroit, Univ. of	9	0	1
Hope College	9	3	4
Kalamazoo College	5	1	2
Michigan College of Mining and Technology	5	2	0
Michigan State University	22	2	7
Michigan, Univ. of	214	17	71
Wayne University	55	4	16
Western Michigan College	11	0	3
MINNESOTA (7)			
Carleton College	34	3	12
Gustavus Adolphus College	5	1	2
Macalester College	9	1	1
Minnesota, Univ. of	98	15	19
Saint Olaf College	6	0	2
MISSISSIPPI (7),			
Millsaps College	8	1	4
Mississippi, Univ. of	10	1	2
MISSOURI (22)			
Concordia Theological Seminary	13	1	3
Drury College	5	0	0
Kansas City, Univ. of	17	1	4
Missouri, Univ. of	47	6	12
Park College	17	2	4
Saint Louis University	12	0	1
Oklahoma City University	6	0	0
Washington University	29	6	5
William Jewell College	9	1	2
MONTANA (2)			
Montana State College	5	0	2
Montana State University	13	5	4

Table 52. INSTITUTIONS SENDING AT LEAST FIVE ALUMNI TO COLUMBIA GRADUATE FACULTIES 1940–56 (*Continued*)

	Total	*Ph.D.'s earned*	*M.A.'s earned*
AMERICAN UNIVERSITIES			
NEBRASKA (11)			
Creighton University	5	0	2
Doane College	5	0	4
Nebraska, University of	25	2	7
Nebraska Wesleyan University	10	1	2
Union College	5	0	2
NEVADA (1)			
NEW HAMPSHIRE (5)			
Dartmouth College	156	20	58
New Hampshire, Univ. of	33	3	7
NEW JERSEY (30)			
Drew University	37	6	6
Fairleigh Dickinson College	7	0	2
Georgian Court College	14	0	5
Newark College of Engineering	16	0	1
Newark Colleges of Rutgers University	13	2	2
New Jersey College for Women	75	1	21
New Jersey State Teachers College (Newark)	5	0	3
New Jersey State Teachers College (Trenton)	13	1	5
New Jersey State Teachers College (Upper Montclair)	114	1	28
Princeton University	183	18	48
Rutgers University	208	13	74
College of Saint Elizabeth	20	1	8
Saint Peter's College	30	2	5
Seton Hall University	39	1	7
Stevens Inst. of Technology	20	1	4
Upsala College	37	2	10
NEW MEXICO (4)			
New Mexico, Univ. of	25	5	7
NEW YORK (104)			
Adelphi College	62	1	15
Alfred University	7	0	1
Bard College	46	4	15
Barnard College	598	30	213
Brooklyn College	1,101	60	315
Brooklyn, Polytechnic Inst. of	42	5	8
Buffalo, Univ. of	38	3	9
Canisius College	6	0	1
College of the City of New York	1,343	151	416
Colgate University	42	1	12
Columbia College	1,172	155	457
Columbia University (General Studies)	612	24	217
Cooper Union	34	5	9
Cornell University	262	24	79
Elmira College	16	1	8
Fordham University	213	11	60

Table 52. INSTITUTIONS SENDING AT LEAST FIVE ALUMNI TO COLUMBIA GRADUATE FACULTIES 1940–56 (*Continued*)

	Total	*Ph.D.'s earned*	*M.A.'s earned*
AMERICAN UNIVERSITIES			
Good Counsel College	18	0	4
Hamilton College	53	5	22
Hartwick College	10	1	3
Hobart College	40	2	15
Hofstra College	89	2	26
Houghton College	16	1	8
Hunter College	1,010	30	269
Iona College	9	1	0
Juilliard School of Music	8	0	4
Keuka College	6	0	2
Long Island University	56	1	26
Manhattan College	83	1	23
Manhattanville College of the Sacred Heart	41	0	18
Marymount College	15	0	4
College of Mount Saint Vincent	46	1	12
Nazareth College	5	0	1
College of New Rochelle	68	2	21
New School for Social Research	29	2	11
State University College for Teachers (Albany)	80	3	16
State University College for Teachers (Buffalo)	11	0	0
State University Teachers College (Oswego)	5	0	0
New York University	767	27	239
Niagara University	8	1	1
Notre Dame College of Staten Island	16	0	4
Pratt Institute	6	0	1
Queens College	317	21	101
Rensselaer Polytechnic Institute	31	6	9
Rochester, Univ. of	84	8	24
Russell Sage College	15	0	6
Saint Bonaventure University	29	0	6
Saint Francis College	16	1	2
Saint John's University	110	5	28
Saint Joseph's College for Women	42	0	14
Saint Joseph's Seminary and College	11	0	0
Saint Lawrence University	25	2	4
Sarah Lawrence College	40	2	3
Siena College	6	1	3
Skidmore College	26	0	9
Syracuse University	158	7	39
Union College and University	58	5	16
United States Military Academy	182	2	60
Vassar College	217	9	75
Wagner Memorial Lutheran College	62	4	15
Webb Inst. of Naval Architecture	7	2	2
Wells College	12	1	3
Yeshiva University	151	8	43

Table 52. INSTITUTIONS SENDING AT LEAST FIVE ALUMNI TO COLUMBIA GRADUATE FACULTIES 1940–56 (*Continued*)

	Total	*Ph.D.'s earned*	*M.A.'s earned*
AMERICAN UNIVERSITIES			
NORTH CAROLINA (31)			
Davidson College	10	1	4
Duke University	74	3	18
Guilford College	8	2	1
Johnson C. Smith University	5	0	2
Meredith College	6	0	2
North Carolina State College of Agriculture and Engineering	11	3	2
North Carolina, Univ. of	98	15	26
Woman's College of the Univ. of North Carolina	16	0	6
Salem College	5	0	2
Wake Forest College	12	0	6
NORTH DAKOTA (3)			
North Dakota, Univ. of	10	0	2
OHIO (44)			
Akron, Univ. of	15	0	3
Antioch College	48	2	18
Baldwin-Wallace College	11	1	2
Bowling Green State University	12	0	4
Case Inst. of Technology	8	1	3
Cincinnati, Univ. of	35	10	12
Denison University	30	4	7
Heidelberg College	5	0	4
Hiram College	8	0	1
Kent State University	19	1	5
Kenyon College	21	0	7
Marietta College	8	0	2
Miami University	10	1	1
Mount Union College	6	0	4
Muskingum College	10	0	1
Oberlin College	120	13	52
Ohio State University	80	6	23
Ohio University	37	2	16
Ohio Wesleyan University	27	3	7
Western College for Women	7	0	1
Western Reserve University	69	4	18
Wittenberg College	6	0	2
The College of Wooster	39	6	18
Xavier University	5	1	2
OKLAHOMA (13)			
Oklahoma A & M College	12	2	2
Oklahoma, Univ. of	42	2	7
Phillips University	6	0	2
Tulsa, Univ. of	9	1	2

Table 52. INSTITUTIONS SENDING AT LEAST FIVE ALUMNI TO COLUMBIA GRADUATE FACULTIES 1940–56 (*Continued*)

	Total	*Ph.D.'s earned*	*M.A.'s earned*
AMERICAN UNIVERSITIES			
OREGON (9)			
Oregon State College	10	1	1
Oregon, Univ. of	17	2	5
Reed College	49	8	16
PENNSYLVANIA (79)			
Albright College	9	1	2
Allegheny College	11	0	2
Beaver College	13	1	1
Bryn Mawr College	96	5	29
Bucknell University	46	1	14
Carnegie Inst. of Technology	17	4	3
Cedar Crest College	8	0	3
Chatham College	6	0	0
Chestnut Hill College	8	0	4
Dickinson College	22	2	7
Drexel Inst. of Technology	6	0	2
Franklin and Marshall College	28	1	12
Gannon College	5	0	1
Geneva College	6	0	1
Gettysburg College	24	0	7
Grove City College	7	0	1
Haverford College	44	3	18
Juniata College	7	0	2
Lafayette College	41	3	18
Lebanon Valley College	19	2	5
Lehigh University	32	6	14
Lincoln University	8	0	3
Marywood College	5	0	0
Moravian College	6	2	0
Muhlenberg College	22	1	11
The Pennsylvania State College	96	10	28
Pennsylvania State Teachers College (Bloomsburg)	6	0	2
Pennsylvania, Univ. of	134	18	31
Pittsburgh, Univ. of	80	9	25
Saint Vincent College	5	0	2
Scranton, Univ. of	13	0	5
Seton Hill College	12	1	3
Susquehanna University	5	0	0
Swarthmore College	126	10	46
Temple University	66	9	21
Thiel College	7	0	3
Ursinus College	24	0	10
Villanova College	10	1	4
Washington and Jefferson College	6	0	0
Waynesburg College	7	1	2
Westminster College	8	1	3
Wilson College	40	3	17

Table 52. INSTITUTIONS SENDING AT LEAST FIVE ALUMNI TO COLUMBIA GRADUATE FACULTIES 1940–56 (*Continued*)

	Total	*Ph.D.'s earned*	*M.A.'s earned*
AMERICAN UNIVERSITIES			
RHODE ISLAND (5)			
Brown University	89	6	35
Pembroke College	6	0	2
Providence College	13	2	2
Rhode Island, Univ. of	6	2	1
SOUTH CAROLINA (21)			
Benedict College	5	2	0
College of Charleston	9	1	2
The Citadel	10	0	3
Converse College	8	0	4
Erskine College	5	1	0
Furman University	12	3	3
South Carolina, Univ. of	33	5	13
Winthrop College	10	1	2
SOUTH DAKOTA (5)			
TENNESSEE (21)			
Chattanooga, Univ. of	6	0	2
Fisk University	9	1	2
Maryville College	12	1	5
Memphis State College	6	1	0
South, Univ. of the	14	1	4
Southwestern at Memphis	12	1	2
Tennessee, Univ. of	14	1	2
Vanderbilt University	28	5	7
TEXAS (38)			
Baylor University	12	1	3
Houston, Univ. of	6	0	2
North Texas State College	13	0	0
Rice Institute	11	1	5
Sam Houston State Teachers College	6	0	1
Southern Methodist University	36	3	14
Texas A & M College	9	0	5
Texas Christian University	16	2	2
Texas State College for Women	11	0	2
Texas Technological College	7	0	1
Texas, Univ. of	103	13	32
UTAH (4)			
Brigham Young University	16	1	8
Utah, Univ. of	33	5	5
VERMONT (6)			
Bennington College	29	1	3
Middlebury College	66	6	20
Saint Michael's College	5	0	0
Univ. of Vermont and State Agricultural College	52	4	18
VIRGINIA (25)			
Hampton Institute	5	0	1
Hollins College	5	0	2

Table 52. INSTITUTIONS SENDING AT LEAST FIVE ALUMNI TO COLUMBIA GRADUATE FACULTIES 1940–56 (*Continued*)

	Total	*Ph.D.'s earned*	*M.A.'s earned*
AMERICAN UNIVERSITIES			
Randolph-Macon College	15	1	3
Randolph-Macon Woman's College	35	0	18
Richmond, Univ. of	33	2	9
Roanoke College	10	0	2
Sweet Briar College	19	0	8
Virginia Military Institute	7	0	5
Virginia Polytechnic Institute	14	1	2
Virginia Union University	7	0	1
Virginia, Univ. of	47	4	12
Washington and Lee University	24	2	8
College of William and Mary	43	1	12
WASHINGTON (11)			
State College of Washington	15	2	4
Washington, Univ. of	104	13	30
Whitman College	15	0	7
WEST VIRGINIA (13)			
Bethany College	14	0	7
Marshall College	9	0	1
West Virginia University	28	0	10
WISCONSIN (15)			
Beloit College	5	0	1
Carroll College	9	0	4
Marquette University	6	0	2
Ripon College	5	0	2
Wisconsin State College (Milwaukee)	5	1	1
Wisconsin, Univ. of	156	8	36
WYOMING (1)			
Wyoming, Univ. of	5	1	1
HAWAII (1)			
Hawaii, Univ. of	30	2	10
PUERTO RICO (3)			
Polytechnic Inst. of Puerto Rico	6	0	2
Puerto Rico, Univ. of	83	5	30
FOREIGN UNIVERSITIES			
AFGANISTAN (1)			
ANGLO-EGYPTIAN SUDAN (1)			
ARGENTINA (6)			
National University of Buenos Aires	8	1	1
AUSTRALIA (5)			
Melbourne, Univ. of	7	2	2
Sydney, Univ. of	6	0	4
AUSTRIA (9)			
Vienna, Univ. of	46	9	8
BELGIUM (9)			
Brussels, Univ. of	20	3	7
Louvain, Univ. of	10	0	4
BOLIVIA (2)			

Table 52. INSTITUTIONS SENDING AT LEAST FIVE ALUMNI TO COLUMBIA GRADUATE FACULTIES 1940–56 (*Continued*)

	Total	*Ph.D.'s earned*	*M.A.'s earned*
FOREIGN UNIVERSITIES			
BRAZIL (15)			
BRITISH WEST INDIES (1)			
BULGARIA (1)			
BURMA (2)			
Rangoon, Univ. of	12	1	5
CANADA (28)			
Arcadia University	6	1	1
Dalhousie University	10	1	2
Laval University	6	0	3
McGill University	45	7	16
McMaster University	16	0	5
Mount Allison University	6	1	3
Queen's University	6	2	3
Alberta, Univ. of	13	5	1
British Columbia, Univ. of	41	6	14
Manitoba, Univ. of	15	2	3
Montreal, Univ. of	12	0	3
Saskatchewan, Univ. of	24	10	7
Toronto, Univ. of	89	14	27
Western Ontario, Univ. of	9	0	6
CHILE (2)			
Chile, Univ. of	5	0	1
CHINA (49)			
Central Inst. of Political Science	7	1	0
Kwang Hua University	6	0	1
Lingnan University	9	2	2
National Central University	29	2	7
National Chekian University	7	0	1
National Chiao-Tung University	8	0	0
National Fuh Tan University	5	0	2
National Peking University	11	2	1
National Southwestern University of China	15	1	5
National Sun Yat-Sen University	10	1	1
National Tsinghua University	20	3	10
National Wuhan University	17	0	5
Saint Joseph's University	25	1	13
Nanking, Univ. of	10	1	0
Shanghai, Univ. of	6	0	3
Yenchian University	25	2	5
COLOMBIA (4)			
CUBA (2)			
Havana, Univ. of	20	0	4
CZECHOSLOVAKIA (8)			
Charles University of Prague	28	2	9
DENMARK (3)			
Copenhagen, Univ. of	10	0	2
DOMINICAN REPUBLIC (1)			

Table 52. INSTITUTIONS SENDING AT LEAST FIVE ALUMNI TO COLUMBIA GRADUATE FACULTIES 1940–56 (*Continued*)

	Total	*Ph.D.'s earned*	*M.A.'s earned*
FOREIGN UNIVERSITIES			
EGYPT (5)			
Egypt, Univ. of	17	3	3
EL SALVADOR (1)			
FINLAND (3)			
Helsinki University	7	0	0
FRANCE (27)			
Paris, Univ. of (Sorbonne)	64	7	10
GERMANY (30)			
Free University of Berlin	7	1	3
Friedrich Wilhelm University of Berlin	10	1	1
Heidelberg, Univ. of	6	2	1
GREAT BRITAIN AND NORTHERN IRELAND (19)			
Birmingham, Univ. of	5	1	3
Cambridge, Univ. of	16	2	6
London, Univ. of	39	7	15
Oxford, Univ. of	19	4	0
GREECE (7)			
National University of Athens	30	0	7
GUATEMALA (2)			
HAITI (1)			
HONG KONG (1)			
HUNGARY (8)			
Péter Pázmány University of Budapest	18	2	3
ICELAND (1)			
INDIA (25)			
Agra University	5	1	2
Benares Hindu University	8	1	2
Patna University	17	2	11
Allahabad, Univ. of	6	0	2
Bombay, Univ. of	44	2	25
Calcutta, Univ. of	19	1	11
Delhi, Univ. of	9	1	4
Madras, Univ. of	16	1	4
INDONESIA (3)			
IRAN (3)			
Tehran, Univ. of	30	1	12
IRAQ (1)			
IRELAND (3)			
ISRAEL (4)			
Hebrew University	23	6	6
ITALY (20)			
Milan, Univ. of	5	0	1
Rome, Univ. of	12	0	4
Turin, Univ. of	5	1	0
JAPAN (23)			
Tokyo University	10	0	1
Toyo University	18	0	3

Table 52. INSTITUTIONS SENDING AT LEAST FIVE ALUMNI TO COLUMBIA GRADUATE FACULTIES 1940–56 (*Continued*)

	Total	*Ph.D.'s earned*	*M.A.'s earned*
FOREIGN UNIVERSITIES			
KOREA (4)			
LEBANON (4)			
American University of Beirut	25	3	6
MEXICO (6)			
Mexico City College	5	0	0
National Autonomous University of Mexico	8	0	2
THE NETHERLANDS (8)			
Amsterdam, Univ. of	9	0	1
NEW ZEALAND (2)			
NICARAGUA (1)			
NORWAY (4)			
Oslo, Univ. of	7	0	0
PAKISTAN (3)			
Panjab, Univ. of	7	2	2
PANAMA (2)			
PARAGUAY (1)			
PERU (3)			
PHILIPPINES (8)			
Philippines, Univ. of	13	0	8
POLAND (14)			
Warsaw, Univ. of	8	4	1
PORTUGAL (1)			
RUMANIA (2)			
SIAM (1)			
SPAIN (7)			
Madrid, Univ. of	9	3	0
SWEDEN (6)			
SWITZERLAND (9)			
Swiss Federal Inst. of Technology	5	1	1
Geneva, Univ. of	8	0	2
Zurich, Univ. of	10	1	1
SYRIA (2)			
TURKEY (8)			
Istanbul, Univ. of	7	0	3
Robert College	13	0	1
Ankara, Univ. of	5	0	3
UNION OF SOUTH AFRICA (6)			
Cape Town, Univ. of	6	1	0
UNION OF SOVIET SOCIALIST REPUBLICS (9)			
VENEZUELA (1)			
Central University of Venezuela	9	0	4
YUGOSLAVIA (3)			
Belgrade, Univ. of	7	1	2

Table 53. STUDENTS ENTERING 1940–56, BY REGIONS OF BIRTH AND SUCCESS IN EARNING PH.D. AND M.A. DEGREES (*In percent*)

		New York City			New England and Middle Atlantic States		
			Degree earned by 1956			Degree earned by 1956	
	Total students entering	Percent of total	Ph.D	M.A.	Percent of total	Ph.D	M.A.
1940–42							
Pure Science	762	36	17	23	27	20	21
Political Science	999	38	8	34	21	9	24
Philosophy	991	29	6	28	28	7	25
1943–45							
Pure Science	769	38	16	26	27	15	33
Political Science	1,175	33	5	30	24	9	23
Philosophy	1,255	30	5	23	26	6	27
1946–48							
Pure Science	1,372	36	28	35	27	24	36
Political Science	2,500	30	8	41	27	12	36
Philosophy	2,252	29	7	39	29	7	43
1949–51							
Pure Science	1,139	34	20	34	26	21	30
Political Science	2,146	30	2	33	25	4	34
Philosophy	2,212	30	2	36	29	3	36
1952–54							
Pure Science	809	34	2	32	23	2	27
Political Science	1,471	29	1	27	22	0	24
Philosophy	1,314	27	0	28	26	0	29
1955–56							
Pure Science	337	43	0	14	0	0	8
Political Science	666	32	0	3	0	0	8
Philosophy	573	35	0	7	0	0	6

* Percentage based on a group smaller than 50.

South, Midwest, and West			Foreign Countries				
Percent of total	Degree earned by 1956		Percent of total	Degree earned by 1956		Total Students entering	
	Ph.D.	M.A.		Ph.D.	M.A.		
							1940–42
20	29	17	17	29	29	762	Pure Science
21	9	22	19	12	27	999	Political Science
24	6	18	18	12	26	991	Philosophy
							1943–45
19	11	30	16	15	22	769	Pure Science
20	10	26	21	8	24	1,175	Political Science
23	7	25	19	11	28	1,255	Philosophy
							1946–48
16	29	31	19	30	28	1,372	Pure Science
21	15	32	21	10	39	2,500	Political Science
27	10	43	13	15	35	2,252	Philosophy
							1949–51
17	16	26	21	21	31	1,139	Pure Science
22	5	34	22	4	38	2,146	Political Science
25	3	36	14	5	34	2,212	Philosophy
							1952–54
17	3	24	24	5	30	809	Pure Science
20	1	28	25	1	35	1,471	Political Science
23	0	25	20	2	33	1,314	Philosophy
							1955–56
1	0 *	17 *	21	0	12	337	Pure Science
0	0	9	26	0	5	666	Political Science
0	0	12	19	0	8	573	Philosophy

Table 54. AGE AT ENTRANCE AND SUCCESS IN EARNING PH.D., NONVETERAN MEN, VETERANS AND WOMEN ENTERING 1940–56 *(In percent)*

		Age at Entrance											
		20 or less			*21–23*			*24–29*			*30 or over*		
	Total students entering	*Nonveteran men*	*Veterans*	*Women*	*Nonveteran men*	*Veterans*	*Women*	*Nonveteran men*	*Veterans*	*Women*	*Nonveteran men*	*Veterans*	*Women*
1940–42													
Pure Science	762	9	26	13	42	46	48	31	29	25	17	0	14
Political Science	998	8	20	15	31	49	47	35	23	21	26	7	17
Philosophy	990	6	9	8	32	50	43	27	30	26	35	11	23
1943–45													
Pure Science	768	14	9	16	30	18	52	32	56	20	24	18	12
Political Science	1,176	7	3	11	25	19	50	34	52	24	34	26	15
Philosophy	1,255	9	4	9	30	20	49	33	53	22	28	24	20
1946–48													
Pure Science	1,371	11	2	13	24	27	52	44	61	24	21	19	11
Political Science	2,497	7	1	8	23	17	44	42	64	33	29	17	15
Philosophy	2,256	9	1	7	28	16	49	40	64	28	23	20	15
1949–51													
Pure Science	1,139	8	0	5	50	19	50	30	65	33	13	16	12
Political Science	2,146	4	0	5	41	14	55	35	59	25	20	27	15
Philosophy	2,212	3	0*	3	47	10	51	32	63	26	18	26	19
1952–54													
Pure Science	807	3	0	9	60	3	45	25	66	33	12	31	12
Political Science	1,471	2	0	3	47	0	55	31	60	27	20	39	15
Philosophy	1,314	2	0	3	56	4	54	29	61	26	13	35	18
1955–56													
Pure Science	337	4	0	5	60	2	42	24	55	27	13	43	26
Political Science	666	3	0	3	40	0	48	34	44	28	23	56	21
Philosophy	573	3	0	3	54	0	50	29	23	27	14	78	20

* Percentage based on a group smaller than 50.

	Ph.D. earned by 1956												
	20 or less			*21–23*			*24–29*			*30 or over*			
	Nonveteran men	*Veterans*	*Women*	*Nonveteran men*	*Veterans*	*Women*	*Nonveteran men*	*Veterans*	*Women*	*Nonveteran men*	*Veterans*	*Women*	*Total students entering*
1940–42													
Pure Science	26 *	100 *	6 *	29	81 *	11	21	70	15	11	0 *	6	762
Political Science	20 *	26 *	5	9	30 *	3	10	23	4	10	0 *	4	998
Philosophy	10 *	20 *	9 *	6	30 *	3	12	44	4	10	0 *	4	990
1943–45													
Pure Science	25 *	0 *	10	24	30 *	12	17	38	8	9	20 *	6	768
Political Science	7 *	0 *	1	17	26 *	4	9	18	5	9	19 *	7	1,176
Philosophy	15 *	0 *	4	15	0 *	3	21	20	3	10	11 *	6	1,255
1946–48													
Pure Science	37 *	44 *	20 *	29	33	11	32	33	18	14	26	4	1,371
Political Science	17 *	25 *	8 *	10	11	2	14	14	4	9	18	3	2,497
Philosophy	11 *	10 *	7	6	7	2	18	13	2	22	13	3	2,256
1949–51													
Pure Science	24 *	0 *	29 *	23	25	9	17	20	12	12	25	11	1,139
Political Science	6 *	0 *	0 *	3	5	1	5	5	2	3	4	2	2,146
Philosophy	0 *	0 *	0 *	2	7	1	3	4	1	2	5	4	2,212
1952–54													
Pure Science	0 *	0 *	0 *	3	0 *	0	8	2	0	17	2 *	0	807
Political Science	0 *	0 *	0 *	0	0 *	0	2	1	0	8	3	0	1,471
Philosophy	0 *	0 *	0 *	0	0 *	1	0	1	0	3	1	0	1,314
1955–56													
Pure Science	0 *	0	0	0	0	0	0 *	0	0	0 *	0	0	337
Political Science	0 *	0	0	0	0	0	0	0	0	0	0	0	666
Philosophy	0 *	0	0	0	0	0	0	0	0	0 *	0	0	573

Table 55. REGISTRATION PATTERNS AND SUCCESS IN EARNING PH.D., STUDENTS ENTERING 1940–51 (*In percent*)

		Students Starting with 2 Consecutive Full-time Semesters			*Students Starting with 1 Full-time and 1 Part-time Semester*		
			Degree earned by 1956			*Degree earned by 1956*	
Department	*Total students entering*	*Percent of total*	*Ph.D.*	*M.A.*	*Percent of total*	*Ph.D.*	*M.A.*
		PURE SCIENCE					
Chemistry	749	55	44	38	10	35	19
Geology	311	64	42	36	5	7 *	33 *
Mathematics	706	37	5	67	7	7 *	35 *
Physics	629	55	28	38	7	20 *	7 *
Psychology	631	46	26	65	9	25	39
Zoology	260	48	32	44	9	9 *	26 *
		POLITICAL SCIENCE					
Anthropology	370	56	24	16	7	16 *	4 *
Economics	1,670	51	11	52	6	5	34
History	1,937	49	15	57	8	7	45
Mathematical Statistics	275	49	12	49	7	0 *	40 *
Public Law	1,538	54	10	49	8	9	33
Sociology	1,030	45	9	36	8	6	31
		PHILOSOPHY					
English	3,716	54	6	56	7	2	45
Fine Arts	191	40	8	42	10	5 *	37 *
French	598	44	6	56	7	2	45
German	131	47	11	52	11	7 *	53 *
Greek and Latin	136	45	11	61	6	13 *	25 *
Music	198	30	0	73	8	0 *	50 *
Philosophy	642	49	21	33	8	16 *	27 *
Religion	318	59	32	15	9	28 *	17 *
Slavic	177	63	16	42	7	0 *	15 *
Spanish	553	31	11	48	5	7 *	33 *

* Percentage based on a group smaller than 50.

Students Starting with 1 Part-time and 1 Full-time Semester			Students Starting with 2 Consecutive Part-time Semesters				
Percent of total	Degree earned by 1956 Ph.D.	Degree earned by 1956 M.A.	Percent of total	Degree earned by 1956 Ph.D.	Degree earned by 1956 M.A.	Students Starting with 1 Full-time Semester and Discontinuing	Students Starting with 1 Part-time Semester and Discontinuing
			PURE SCIENCE				
3	54 *	8 *	12	20	22	6	10
9	44 *	22 *	9	3 *	55 *	4	9
4	8 *	58 *	33	2	38	3	13
6	21 *	26 *	15	9	23	4	11
4	26 *	43 *	16	13	34	4	19
8	38 *	43 *	15	8 *	31 *	10	10
			POLITICAL SCIENCE				
4	15 *	23 *	16	8	14	5	12
3	8	48	19	4	22	5	14
3	24	38	23	4	30	4	9
1	33 *	33 *	22	5	23	4	13
3	5 *	30 *	16	2	23	7	9
2	16 *	40 *	24	3	18	5	13
			PHILOSOPHY				
3	0	50	19	3	22	5	8
4	13 *	38 *	25	0 *	20 *	4	14
3	38 *	38 *	24	11	17	4	11
3	0 *	50 *	24	3 *	13 *	5	6
8	0 *	100 *	35	2 *	27 *	1	6
6	0 *	55 *	37	9	38	3	14
3	25 *	15 *	21	7	12	7	10
3	20 *	0 *	20	14	14	2	5
5	0 *	13 *	12	14 *	14 *	3	7
4	0 *	41 *	37	2	18	4	14

Table 56. YEARS SPENT BY STUDENTS EARNING PH.D. DEGREES AWARDED 1940–56

Department	Total awarded	Average time in years	Time Spans (percentage of students) 1–3 years	4–5 years	6–7 years	8–9 years	10–11 years	12–13 years	14–15 years	16 years and over		
PURE SCIENCE												
Anatomy	15	6.3	27 *	33 *	13 *	7 *	7 *	7 *	0 *	7 *		
Astronomy	6	7.5	0 *	17 *	33 *	17 *	33 *	0 *	0 *	0 *		
Biochemistry	61	5.7	12	43	31	8	3	0	2	2		
Botany	53	6.6	17	42	13	8	4	4	9	4		
Chemistry	345	5.3	18	48	20	6	4	1	1	1		
Geology	139	6.6	19	31	20	12	6	4	6	2		
Mathematics	44	7.4	18 *	23 *	25 *	11 *	2 *	7 *	5 *	9 *		
Microbiology	20	7.1	10 *	25 *	25 *	20 *	10 *	5 *	0 *	5 *		
Pharmacology	3	5.7	33 *	67 *	0	0	0	0	0	0		
Physics	142	7.0	5	33	37	13	4	4	1	4		
Physiology	18	5.4	28 *	44 *	17 *	0 *	6 *	0 *	0 *	6 *		
Psychology	157	5.5	28	38	18	7	1	3	3	3		
Zoology	73	6.5	8	30	32	21	5	1	3	0		
POLITICAL SCIENCE												
Anthropology	86	7.5	14	26	16	19	13	5	3	4		
Economics	208	8.8	4	20	23	23	10	7	5	9		
History	329	9.5	4	20	23	16	10	10	4	14		
Mathematical Statistics	25	6.6	16 *	28 *	28 *	12 *	4 *	4 *	4 *	4 *		
Public Law	149	8.1	11	24	23	13	9	5	5	9		
Sociology	102	10.1	3	15	21	15	15	13	10	10		
PHILOSOPHY										16–17 years	18–19 years	20 years and over
Chinese and Japanese	21	7.6	5 *	24 *	29 *	24 *	5 *	5 *	5 *	5 *	0 *	
English	255	10.1	2	13	19	23	15	6	9	4	3	7
Fine Arts	15	10.8	7 *	0 *	27 *	13 *	20 *	13 *	0 *	7 *	0 *	13 *
French	142	9.7	7	16	20	16	9	13	5	6	3	6
German	34	12.5	0 *	15 *	12 *	9 *	15 *	15 *	6 *	6 *	9 *	15 *
Greek and Latin	18	10.9	6 *	11 *	6 *	22 *	11 *	11 *	11 *	6 *	11 *	6 *
Italian	15	9.4	7 *	27 *	7 *	13 *	13 *	7 *	13 *	13 *	0 *	0 *
Linguistics	4	5.8	25 *	50 *	0	0	25 *	0	0	0	0	0
Music	9	8.1	0	11 *	11 *	67 *	11 *	0	0	0	0	0
Philosophy	131	7.4	15	26	26	8	8	6	4	1	2	3
Religion	86	5.4	25	36	16	17	1	1	0	1	0	1
Semitic	6	9.7	17 *	17 *	17 *	0	0	0	50 *	0	0	0
Slavic	26	6.2	15 *	31 *	35 *	12 *	0	4 *	0	0	4 *	0
Spanish	41	9.9	10 *	12 *	15 *	17 *	10 *	10 *	12 *	7 *	2 *	5 *

* Percentages based on a group smaller than 50.

Table 57. TIME SPANS IN YEARS BETWEEN ENTRANCE AND AWARDING OF PH.D BY AGE-AT-ENTRANCE GROUPS

Age at entrance	*10 percent sample 182 Ph.D.'s before 1940*	*Pure Science 1,219 Ph.D.'s 1941–56*	*Political Science 899 Ph.D.'s 1941–56*	*Philosophy 718 Ph.D.'s 1941–56*
17	. . .	8.7 *	9.7 *	. . .
18	. . .	7.3 *	4.0 *	7.4 *
19	6.0 *	6.2 *	10.5 *	12.8 *
20	5.2 *	6.9	10.2 *	11.2 *
21	9.0 *	6.4	10.2	12.3
22	8.2 *	6.4	9.7	10.9
23	7.5 *	6.0	9.8	9.8
24	8.3 *	6.1	9.4	9.0
25	10.0 *	5.6	7.9	8.8
26	7.8 *	5.3	8.1	9.1
27	6.7 *	4.9	7.2	9.4 *
28	9.6 *	5.3	8.2 *	8.8 *
29	12.5 *	5.3 *	8.5 *	7.7 *
30–39	9.1 *	5.4	7.2	7.6

* Average based on less than 50 individual cases.

Table 58. TOTAL ENROLLMENT OF VETERANS UNDER PROVISIONS OF PUBLIC LAWS 346 AND 16

Term		*New students entering under*		*Total veterans enrolled in the Graduate Faculties*	*Total veterans enrolled in Columbia*
		Public Law 346	*Public Law 16*		
1946–47	Winter	732	67	1,840	10,456
	Spring	214	94	1,857	10,687
1947–48	Winter	503	116	2,053	11,332
	Spring	92	114	2,031	10,746
1948–49	Winter	416	75	2,154	10,071
	Spring	108	57	2,051	9,308
1949–50	Winter	400	66	2,347	8,921
	Spring	77	57	2,301	8,082
1950–51	Winter	448	30	1,902	6,641
	Spring	134	29	1,739	6,334
1951–52	Winter *	62	18	1,353	5,019
	Spring	17	15	1,104	4,198
1952–53	Winter	26	8	668	2,985
	Spring	10	4	526	2,484
1953–54	Winter	33	2	352	1,837
	Spring	2	1	294	1,417
1954–55	Winter	7	4	202	1,038
	Spring	0	6	172	846
1955–56	Winter	0	3	133	582
	Spring	0	2	105	445

* Deadline for enrollment under P.L. 346 for those discharged by July 25, 1947.

Table 59. DEGREES EARNED BY 1956 BY NONVETERAN MEN, VETERANS, AND WOMEN ENTERING 1940–51

		Nonveteran Men			*Veterans*			*Women*		
Department	*Total students entering 1940–51*	*Percent of total*	*Percent with Ph.D. by 1956*	*Percent with M.A. by 1956*	*Percent of total*	*Percent with Ph.D. by 1956*	*Percent with M.A. by 1956*	*Percent of total*	*Percent with Ph.D. by 1956*	*Percent with M.A. by 1956*
PURE SCIENCE										
Chemistry	749	48	34	25	28	42	30	24	19	26
Geology	311	45	31	29	41	39	29	12	3 *	58 *
Mathematics	706	41	5	37	26	5	47	33	0	42
Physics	629	50	18	22	40	23	32	9	9	25
Psychology	631	33	18	38	20	33	43	46	10	41
Zoology	260	37	24	30	21	31	27	42	12	38
POLITICAL SCIENCE										
Anthropology	370	28	18	11	26	23	7	46	11	15
Economics	1,670	39	6	33	34	12	40	26	2	30
History	1,937	30	12	36	38	13	41	31	3	41
Mathematical Statistics	275	40	9	35	43	7	33	16	5	20 *
Public Law	1,538	35	6	31	39	10	35	25	2	37
Sociology	1,030	29	9	21	31	8	28	39	2	23
PHILOSOPHY										
English	3,716	21	5	38	34	7	47	44	2	32
Fine Arts	191	19	3 *	16	24	9 *	38	57	3	26
French	598	22	19	20	22	21	28	56	8	28
Music	198	27	9	43	26	2	65	46	1	30
Philosophy	642	42	15	21	33	19	22	22	4	16
Religion	318	62	31	7	21	24	9	17	4	40
Spanish	553	20	7	26	19	7	31	61	3	23

* Percentage based on a group smaller than 50.

Table 60. DEGREES EARNED BY 1956 BY STUDENTS ENTERING 1940–51

Department	*1940*			*1941*			*1942*			*1943*		
	Total entering	*M.A. earned by 1956*	*Ph.D. earned by 1956*	*Total entering*	*M.A. earned by 1956*	*Ph.D. earned by 1956*	*Total entering*	*M.A. earned by 1956*	*Ph.D. earned by 1956*	*Total entering*	*M.A. earned by 1956*	*Ph.D. earned by 1956*
PURE SCIENCE												
Chemistry	54	7	18	59	9	25	45	6	19	48	14	10
Geology	18	6	6	11	2	4	12	1	3	8	3	..
Mathematics	44	16	0	30	6	3	23	8	3	40	16	2
Physics	30	4	5	19	2	2	32	8	5	14	2	1
Psychology	86	29	12	82	24	13	49	14	5	43	15	5
Zoology	15	4	3	20	3	5	12	3	1	15	4	1
POLITICAL SCIENCE												
Anthropology	19	1	6	16	..	3	22	2	6	14	2	2
Economics	119	32	12	133	30	7	68	29	2	75	19	6
History	93	32	10	79	30	11	74	24	5	92	26	9
Mathematical Statistics	3	3	0	2	1	1	2	1	..	13	1	2
Public Law	80	24	4	53	15	3	47	12	6	44	8	2
Sociology	71	19	3	67	13	7	51	10	6	51	5	6
PHILOSOPHY												
English	213	63	8	171	35	7	95	24	7	124	27	4
Fine Arts	14	3	0	14	2	2	6	2	..	9	2	1
French	67	14	5	37	9	5	26	5	5	27	6	4
German	18	6	0	6	2	1	4	2	..	9	1	2
Greek and Latin	12	9	0	18	4	2	7	1	..	6	2	..
Music	17	7	1	11	..	1	13	3	1	12	3	..
Philosophy	21	3	9	26	1	1	15	1	4	32	9	3
Religion	...	..	..	8	3	1	10	3	3	16	1	7
Slavic	3	0	0	2	2	..	7	..	1	6	2	1
Spanish	35	8	4	30	7	3	32	4	1	35	7	2

Table 60. DEGREES EARNED BY 1956 BY STUDENTS ENTERING 1940–51 *(Continued)*

Department	1944			1945			1946			1947		
	Total entering	*M.A. earned by 1956*	*Ph.D. earned by 1956*	*Total entering*	*M.A. earned by 1956*	*Ph.D. earned by 1956*	*Total entering*	*M.A. earned by 1956*	*Ph.D. earned by 1956*	*Total entering*	*M.A. earned by 1956*	*Ph.D. earned by 1956*
PURE SCIENCE												
Chemistry	55	8	15	68	19	12	95	30	37	86	30	24
Geology	11	3	2	15	9	4	56	15	22	36	17	10
Mathematics	44	13	2	67	27	1	108	44	7	81	45	3
Physics	25	5	5	40	7	7	104	32	36	98	38	22
Psychology	53	18	2	73	32	10	52	21	17	43	25	9
Zoology	25	6	3	21	4	3	29	8	10	25	9	5
POLITICAL SCIENCE												
Anthropology	19	2	2	26	1	6	54	9	12	37	5	4
Economics	109	30	4	136	48	6	296	104	41	192	86	19
History	127	37	12	132	49	17	304	125	56	215	101	23
Mathematical Statistics	10	3	2	13	2	..	43	15	7	29	14	2
Public Law	52	13	2	103	29	9	241	93	20	171	50	17
Sociology	69	16	3	90	20	2	135	39	11	84	26	4
PHILOSOPHY												
English	224	65	12	233	77	11	499	214	41	462	234	27
Fine Arts	15	5	..	13	2	1	15	4	..	16	4	..
French	43	8	8	50	15	7	74	21	17	54	20	10
German	7	4	1	9	3	..	10	2	1	11	4	..
Greek and Latin	11	5	1	11	4	2	22	9	1	6	1	1
Music	15	4	1	23	7	..	24	9	2	10	8	..
Philosophy	38	5	8	43	3	6	71	16	15	75	21	15
Religion	22	2	10	33	4	6	50	2	17	35	4	9
Slavic	13	1	1	12	3	2	41	15	10	21	5	4
Spanish	57	14	2	69	17	1	65	15	5	51	20	2

Table 60. DEGREES EARNED BY 1956 BY STUDENTS ENTERING 1940–51 (*Continued*)

Department	*1948*			*1949*			*1950*			*1951*		
	Total entering	M.A. earned by 1956	Ph.D. earned by 1956	Total entering	M.A. earned by 1956	Ph.D. earned by 1956	Total entering	M.A. earned by 1956	Ph.D. earned by 1956	Total entering	M.A. earned by 1956	Ph.D. earned by 1956
PURE SCIENCE												
Chemistry	65	18	26	65	18	20	56	24	17	53	15	21
Geology	20	6	7	48	12	18	40	14	12	36	12	10
Mathematics	76	40	1	69	38	2	72	27	1	51	13	..
Physics	69	18	14	91	28	4	66	17	4	41	7	6
Psychology	32	15	11	30	14	10	42	28	9	46	19	7
Zoology	33	13	7	22	9	7	20	10	6	23	12	2
POLITICAL SCIENCE												
Anthropology	29	3	6	42	7	7	49	6	5	43	7	1
Economics	169	66	6	149	60	9	122	40	2	102	36	2
History	180	86	20	233	108	16	228	102	4	180	60	1
Mathematical Statistics	45	20	3	33	8	1	43	10	2	39	11	..
Public Law	178	66	17	203	92	8	177	60	8	189	63	4
Sociology	98	25	9	116	38	4	102	21	1	96	18	4
PHILOSOPHY												
English	355	176	15	514	255	7	466	159	9	360	115	2
Fine Arts	22	6	2	26	8	1	25	10	1	16	4	..
French	47	11	8	64	14	8	51	15	4	58	18	..
German	15	5	1	21	12	1	11	5	..	10	..	2
Greek and Latin	16	5	2	6	5	..	12	8	..	9	1	..
Music	19	13	1	13	9	..	15	11	..	26	11	..
Philosophy	70	14	9	86	18	10	87	23	4	78	22	3
Religion	26	2	7	31	2	8	32	8	2	55	11	8
Slavic	21	7	1	22	8	1	14	6	..	15	4	..
Spanish	60	17	2	53	8	2	35	10	1	31	11	..